MW00789096

Tang Soo Do

The ultimate guide to the Korean martial art

Grand Master Kang Uk Lee

A&C Black • London

Grand Master Kang Uk Lee

First published 1998 by
A & C Black (Publishers) Ltd
35 Bedford Row, London WC1R 4JH

First U.S. edition published 1999 by
Unique Publications
4201 Vanowen Place
Burbank, California 91505

Copyright © by
Grand Master Kang Uk Lee 1998

ISBN 0-86568-170-8

All rights reserved. No part of this publication may be
reproduced in any form or by any means—graphic, electronic
or mechanical, including photocopying, recording, taping or
information storage and retrieval systems—without the prior
permission in writing of the publishers.

A CIP catalogue record for this book is available from the
British Library.

Acknowledgements
All sequence photography by Martin Sellars.

Designed and typeset by
Alan Hamp @ Design for Books

Contents

Foreword

I would like to express my great pleasure in being able to publish this Tang Soo Do book. It has taken a lot of time and hard work, not only from myself but also from the members of the International Tang Soo (Soo Bahk) Do Federation Moo Duk Kwan who contributed to the book.

There are hundreds of thousands of Tang Soo Do practitioners throughout the world and after many years of careful consideration I decided that publishing a Tang Soo Do book would benefit all of these loyal members. This book was produced to meet a clear need expressed by many instructors and students for a series of concise summaries or overviews of Tang Soo Do principles, concepts, inspirations and techniques. It is not a textbook or reader which needs to be studied from cover to cover, but a work of reference for those wishing to familiarise or refamiliarise themselves with the essence of a particular aspect of Tang Soo Do.

I spent many years researching the background and history of Tang Soo Do to illustrate this book; the books from which some pictures are extracted are listed in the bibliography. I hope this book will help all the practitioners who are serious about learning Tang Soo Do to improve their techniques. I also think this book will allow the practitioners worldwide to unite in the traditional practice of Tang Soo Do.

I wish to thank the members who so wholeheartedly offered their help, especially Master Peter V M Chin who spent many sleepless nights working with me on this book and editing the texts. My thanks also to Y M Lee, P Ogborne, J Meakins, F Chin, A Chin, P Amouret, N Watkins, M Shapland and P Barr.

With the family tree, I have tried to show the generations of Tang Soo Do and have received help from many Tang Soo Do Instructors throughout the world. However, I wish to apologise to those who may have been overlooked and to those I could not fit in due to space constraint. I will be grateful for any advice so that mistakes can be corrected in future editions.

Thank you for all the help and encouragement I have received throughout the creation of this book.

Grand Master Kang Uk Lee
President
International Tang Soo (Soo Bahk) Do Federation
Moo Duk Kwan.

Biography of Grand Master Kang Uk Lee

Born	24 August 1936 in Seoul, South Korea.	
1949	Joined Moo Duk Kwan	
1952	1st Dan	
1953	2nd Dan	
1955	3rd Dan	
1956	Tang Soo Do Instructor (Moo Duk Kwan)	Military Police Headquarters, Seoul Ma Po Gymnasium, Seoul Kon Gook (Jong Chi) University, Seoul
1957 to 1962	Tang Soo Do Instructor (Moo Duk Kwan)	Korean Air Force Academy, Jin Hae City / Seoul
1958	4th Dan	
1961	5th Dan	
1962 to 1964	Tang Soo Do Instructor (Moo Duk Kwan)	Ma Po Gymnasium, Seoul
1965	6th Dan	
1964 to 1972	Chief Instructor of the Central Moo Duk Kwan Gymnasium and Director of the Korean Soo Bahk Do Association	
1968	Chief Judge of the 1st World Tang Soo Do and 5th Asia Tang Soo Do Championships, Seoul	
1972	7th Dan	
1972	Chief Instructor for South East Asia, based in Malaysia	
1973	Founded	Brunei Tang Soo Do Association Singapore Tang Soo Do Association
1974	Founded	Federation of Malaysia Tang Soo Do Organisation United Kingdom Tang Soo (Soo Bahk) Do Federation
	Chief Instructor of the United Kingdom Tang Soo (Soo Bahk) Do Federation	

1975	President and Chief Instructor of the United Kingdom Tang Soo (Soo Bahk) Do Federation
1976	Founded European Tang Soo (Soo Bahk) Do Federation, dissolved in 1989
	President and Chief Judge of the 1st European Tang Soo (Soo Bahk) Do Championships
1978	President and Chief Judge of the 1st International Tang Soo (Soo Bahk) Do Championships, United Kingdom
1979	8th Dan
1982	President and Chief Judge of the 2nd International Tang Soo (Soo Bahk) Do Championships, U.S.A.
1989	President and Chief Judge of the 3rd International Tang Soo (Soo Bahk) Do Championships, Korea
1989	Founded International Tang Soo (Soo Bahk) Do Federation Moo Duk Kwan
	President and Chief Instructor of the International Tang Soo (Soo Bahk) Do Federation Moo Duk Kwan
1989	9th Dan
1991	President and Chief Judge of the 4th International Tang Soo (Soo Bahk) Do Championships, United Kingdom
1993	Presented with the Freedom of Jacksonville City, U.S.A.
1993	President and Chief Judge of the 5th International Tang Soo (Soo Bahk) Do Championships, Greece
1995	President and Chief Judge of the 6th International Tang Soo (Soo Bahk) Do Championships, U.S.A.
1997	President and Chief Judge of the 7th International Tang Soo (Soo Bahk) Do Championships, Malaysia

History of Tang Soo Do (Soo Bahk Kee)

It could be said that martial arts originate from the dawn of human existence, when one's very survival depended on the ability to defend oneself.

In primitive times all cultures used traditional unarmed combat skills when fighting tribal wars and as self-defence against animal attacks; these methods of self-defence eventually developed into unique hand and foot skills.

However, the origins of Tang Soo Do as we know it can be traced to the period of the Three Kingdoms in Korea, Shilla 57 BC–935 AD, Paekjae 18 BC–660 AD, and Koguryo 37 BC–668 AD. Many relics of Tang Soo Do (Soo Bahk Kee) from this era survive to the present day. One of the best known examples is the Koguryo wall painting depicting martial arts, which is at least 1500 years old. It was found in Jip Han Yern, on the lower part of the Ap Lok river which forms part of the border between Korea and China. Koguryo murals of the royal tomb reveal the lifestyle of the time; one of the murals excavated during the period 1935–40 depicts a scene in which two warriors are engaged in a hand to hand fight in Tang Soo Do.

Many Shilla Buddhist sculptures, depicting monks practising martial arts, also survive in Korea. The guardians carved at the entrance of Sokkuram Grotto display postures similar to those found in Tang Soo Do.

An entry in the 18th volume of the *History of Koryo*, written

5th century Koguryo Kingdom

5th century Koguryo Kingdom

5th century Koguryo Kingdom

about 800 years ago, mentions We Moon Lee who was appointed to the post of army commander by King E Jong, the 16th king of the Koryo dynasty (918 AD–1392 AD), for his expertise in Tang Soo Do (Soo Bahk Kee). The Koryo army used Tang Soo Do as a combat technique as well as a form of fitness training.

Moo Ye Do Bo, one of the most influential books on martial arts in Korea, was written approximately 500 years ago during the Yi Dynasty and describes various martial arts techniques.

The books increased the popularity of Tang Soo Do (Soo Bahk Kee) among the general public and the army began to use Tang Soo Do competitions as a method of recruiting soldiers.

Modern Tang Soo Do is heavily indebted to Grand Master Hwang Kee who founded the Moo Duk Kwan (Korean Martial Art Academy) on 9th November 1945.

9th century Shilla Kingdom

Kang Uk Lee, now 9th Dan and one of Grand Master Hwang Kee's most senior students, introduced Tang Soo Do to the United Kingdom and

8th century Shilla Kingdom

Bul Kup Sa Temple in Kyongju is one of the oldest and grandest temples in Korea

*8th century
Shilla Kingdom*

*Kum Kang Yuk
Sa Sang*

*8th century
Shilla Kingdom*

South East Asia in the early 1970s. His inspiration and guidance were instrumental in the increase in popularity and development of Tang Soo Do in Europe.

Aw Jong Moo Ye Do Bo Tong Jee (Kwon Bop Pyun)

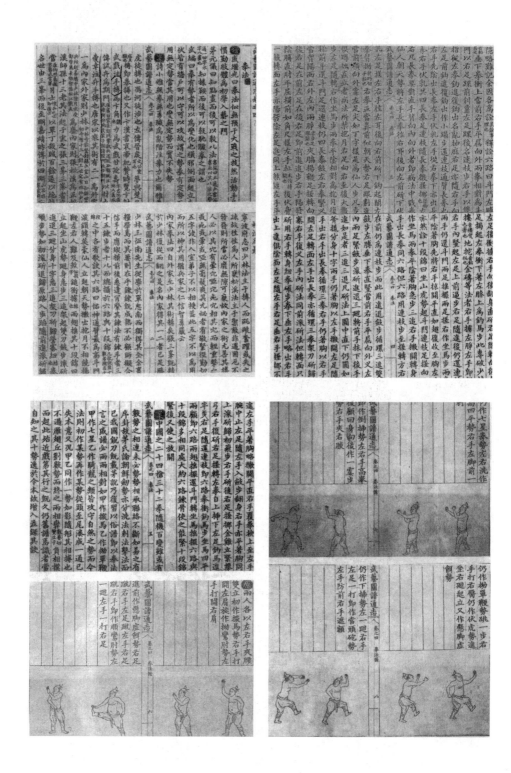

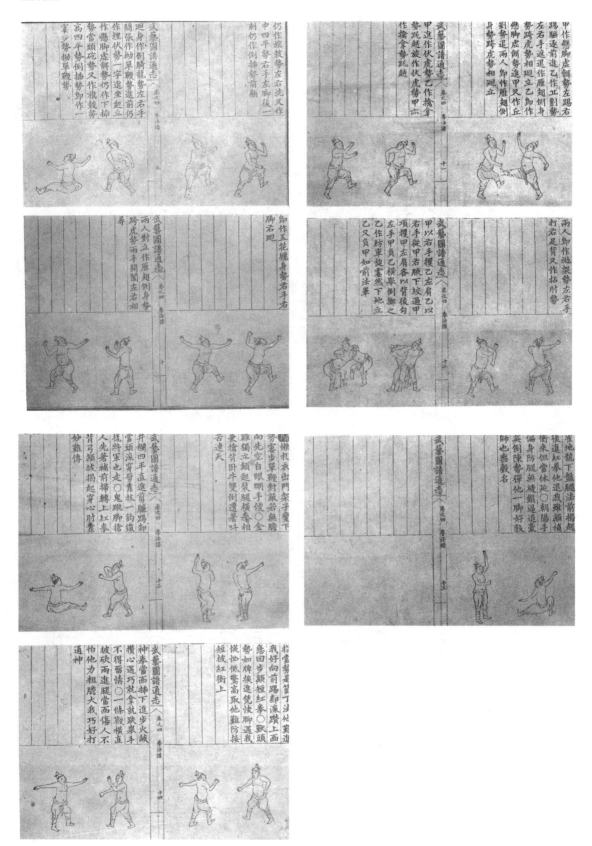

Genealogy of Korean past

Club	Founder	Headquarters					
Moo Duk Kwan	Mr Hwang Kee	Seoul	Moo Duk Kwan	Mr Hwang Kee	Seoul	International Tang Soo (Soo Bahk) Do Federation (United Kingdom)	M Kang Uk Lee
			Moo Duk Kwan			Korean Soo Bahk Do Association (Korea) - 30 June 1960 Registered with Korean Government - Ji Do Kwan joined Soo Bahk Do Association	Mr Hwang Kee
						World Moo Duk Kwan TSD Association (U.S.A.)	Mr Kim Jae Jun
						World Tang Soo Do Federation (U.S.A.)	Mr Shin Jea Chul
			Moo Duk Kwan (Tae Kwon Do)	Mr Lee Kang Eek, Mr Hong Song Soo, Mr Choi Nam Do	Seoul	Tae Kwon Do Association. In 1964 joined Korean Amateur Sports Association and changed its name to Tae Soo Do Association. In 1965 Tae Soo Do Association changed its name to Tae Kwon Do	
Yeun Moo Kwan (Yun Ke Byung)	Mr Chun	Seoul	Ji Do Kwan	Dr Yun Ke Byung	Seoul	Han Moo Kwan, Han Che Gym ", Yun Moo Kwan "	
YMCA Kwon Bop Boo	Mr Yun Byung In	Seoul	Chang Moo Kwan	Mr Lee Nam Suk	Seoul	Kang Duk Won, Chung Moo Kwan ", Kang Moo Kwan "	
Chung Do Kwan	Mr Lee Won Kuk	Seoul	Chung Do Kwan	Mr Son Duk Song, Mr Om In Kyu	Seoul	Oh Do Kwan, Kuk Moo Kwan ", Chung Yong Kwan ", Chung Do Kwan "	
Song Moo Kwan	Mr No Byung Gik	Ke Sung City	Song Moo Kwan	Mr No Byung Jik	Seoul		

Moo Duk Kwan family tree

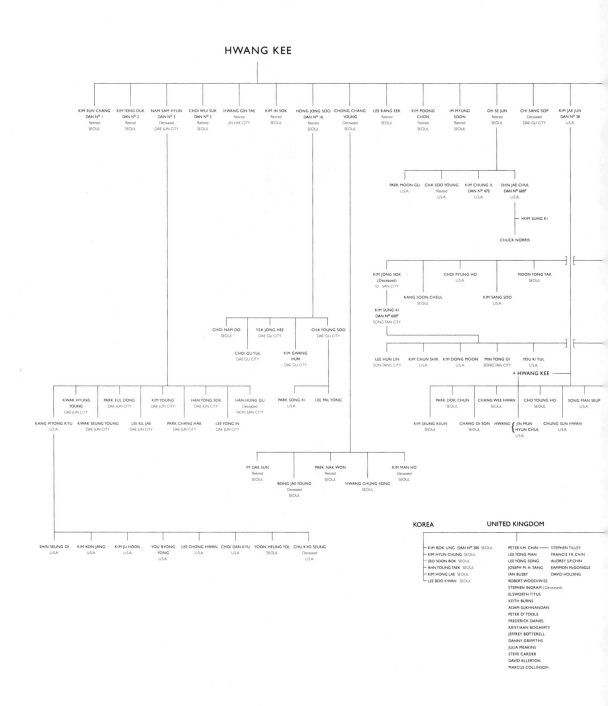

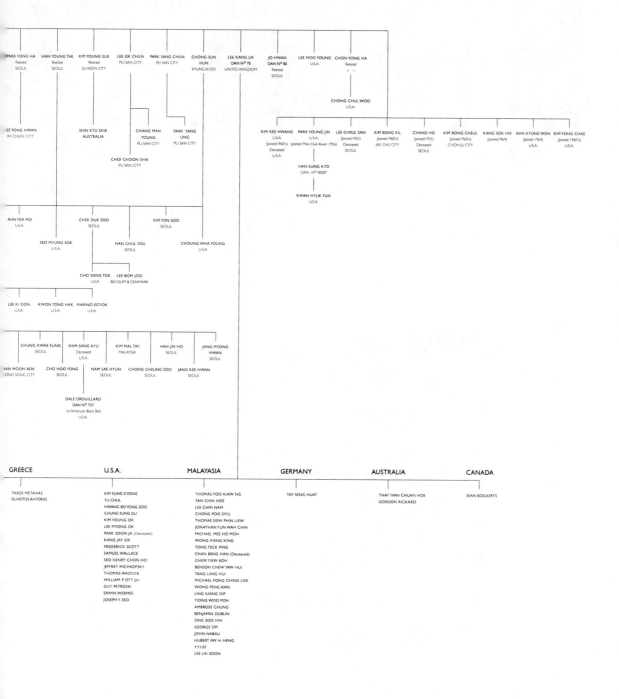

Group photograph taken at Yong San Gym, Seoul (1952)

(l-r): Kang Uk Lee, Hwang Kee, Pak Song Ki (1968)

Certificate presentation by Hwang Kee witnessed by Kang Uk Lee and Consular representatives from the Philippines, at Central Gym, Seoul (1968)

The Korean Ambassador to Malaysia, Dr. Kim Song Yong, visiting the Malaysian Central Gymnasium (17 June, 1973)

Kang Uk Lee proudly displaying the Key of Freedom to Jacksonville City, Florida after the presentation by the Mayor of the city

The British team and officials with their trophies and medals during the 6th International Tang Soo Do Championships in Philadelphia (October, 1995)

Grand Master Kang Uk Lee presenting the 6th Dan Black belt certificate to the Vice-President of East Malaysia, Master Tan Ching Ho (1993)

Grand Master Kang Uk Lee presenting a memento to the Finance and Public Utilities Minister, Datuk Dr. George Chan, during the 6th Malaysian Tang Soo Do Championships in East Malaysia (16 July, 1995)

Presentation of the 1st Dan certificate to the Commander of the Malaysian armed forces region 2, Major General Datuk Mahmood Sulaiman

Group of team members with Grand Master Kang Uk Lee in Athens, Greece during the 5th International Tang Soo Do Championships (1993)
(l-r): Masters A Sukhnandan, P S Chong, M H Moh, C N Lee, J M H Tang, T Metaxas, S H Tay, P V M Chin, K U Lee, A Tsolakis, T F K Ng, F Scott, R Woodiwiss, E Titus, J Y H Chin, K Burns, S Wallaca, G Rickard

Photograph taken during the Masters' course held in Watford Leisure Centre, Watford, Hertfordshire, UK
(Seated l-r): I C Busby, J M H Tang, S H Tay, P V M Chin, K U Lee, T Metaxas, R Woodiwiss, N Zouraris
(Standing l-r): E Titus, D Griffiths, A Sukhnandan, K Burns, P O'Toole, C Bougarts, J Meakins, S Tilley, S Carder, F Chin

Photograph taken during the Black belt course held at Watford Leisure Centre, Watford, Hertfordshire, UK (1995)

Photograph taken during the 15th National Tang Soo Do Championships held in the Bunyan Centre, Bedford, UK (1995)

Outdoor Tang Soo Do training session conducted by Kang Uk Lee for senior police officers at Police Headquarters in Kuching, East Malaysia (1973)

Hand and foot techniques

Hand techniques

Jung Kwon - fist

How to make a fist.

Start with open hand (**fig. 1**), roll the fingers tight towards the palm (**fig. 2**) and finally bring the thumb tightly against the fingers (**fig. 3**).

Figure 1

Figure 2

Figure 3

Kap Kwon - back fist

A back fist is made in the same way as a forefist, but the striking area is at the back of the fist (**fig. 4**). This technique requires accuracy during training, especially if the student is attempting to perform a breaking technique. The contact points are on the back of the first and second knuckles. Application as **fig. 5**.

Figure 4

Figure 5

Yoo Kwon - soft fist

The soft fist, so-called because it is
held loosely, is used for attacks to
the face. It can also be used as a
defensive technique. Use a similar
method to Jung Kwon (figs 1–3) to
make the soft fist.

Figure 6

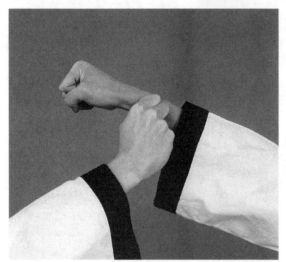

Figure 7

Figure 8

Il Ji Kwon - one finger
fist (with forefinger)

Follow the same method as Jung
Kwon, with the forefinger
positioned forward and the thumb
sitting on top of the forefinger
(fig. 9).

Figure 9

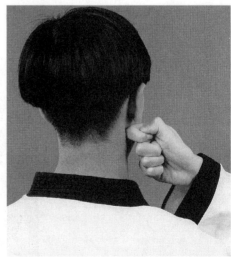

Figure 10

Il Ji Kwon - one finger fist
(with middle finger)

Follow the same method as Jung Kwon, with the middle finger positioned forwards and the thumb tightly placed on top of your fingers (fig. 11).

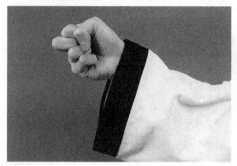

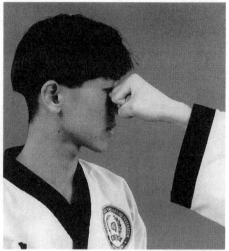

Figure 11

Figure 12

Soo Do - knife hand

How to make a Soo Do hand.

The knife hand techniques are important weapons for Tang Soo Do practitioners; they are used as much as the forefist. The author advises practitioners to take extra care while practising with these techniques, in particular to condition your hand properly before attempting to use Soo Do hand for striking objects; remember to keep your fingers closed tightly together (fig. 14).

With open palm, bend your thumb and then slightly bend the end of the rest of the four fingers (fig. 13), then close the fingers together (fig. 14). The striking area of the Soo Do hand is the area between the wrist and 1cm from the first joint of the little finger.

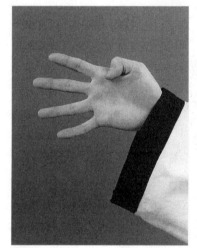

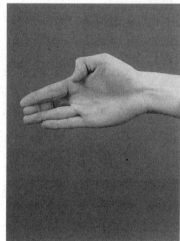

Figure 13

Figure 14

Yuk Soo Do - reverse knife hand

The conditioning of the reverse knife hand is the same as that of the knife hand, but the striking area is on the opposite edge of the knife hand between the forefinger and the thumb muscle. It is mainly used for defence (blocking) but can also be used for offensive purposes.

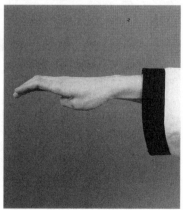

Figure 15

Figure 16

Kwan Soo - spear hand

The spear hand is made in the same way as the knife hand but the application is from a different position. Kwan Soo means 'four fingers hand' and it is usually used for offensive purposes.

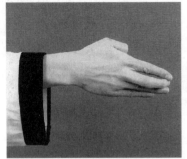

Figure 17

Il Ji Kwan Soo - one finger spear hand

This technique is usually used for attacking weak areas, for example the eyes. The striking area is the tip of the forefinger.

Figure 18

Figure 19

E Ji Kwan Soo - two finger spear hand

Similar to the one finger spear hand, the two finger spear hand is usually used for attacking weak areas such as the eyes. The striking area is the tip of the fore- and second fingers.

Figure 20

Figure 21

Ban Jul Kwan Soo - foreknuckle hand

The foreknuckle hand is used for attacking narrow targets. The striking area is between the knuckle of the fore-, middle and third fingers. This technique is seldom used.

Figure 22

Jip Kye Shon - plier hand

This technique can be used for offensive and defensive moves, for example attacking the throat area (fig. 24) or for blocking or grabbing purposes (fig. 25). The striking area is between the forefinger and the thumb (fig. 23). The four fingers and thumb are slightly bent. This technique is seldom used.

Figure 24

Figure 23

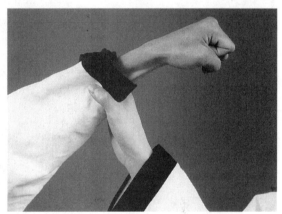

Figure 25

Son Ba Dak Mit (Jang Kwon) - palm heel

This technique can be used for offensive and defensive moves, for example attacks to the jaw in an upper-cut direction or for blocking a strike (fig. 27). The striking area is the heel of the palm (fig. 26). Remember to bend the four fingers and the thumb as illustrated.

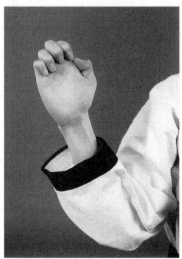

Figure 26

Figure 27

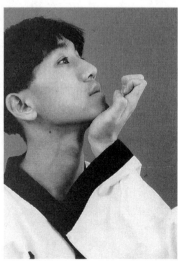

Figure 28

Son Mok Deung - upper wrist technique

This technique is used for offensive and defensive moves. The striking area is the upper wrist, however the technique is seldom used.

Figure 30

Figure 29

Figure 31

Pal Mok - wrist

This technique is one of the strongest and most common blocking areas in Tang Soo Do. It can also be used for attacking.

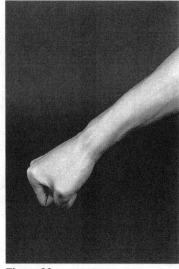

Figure 32

Figure 33

Foot techniques

Bal Ba Dak Mit - palm foot (outside to inside blocking kick)

An outside-inside kicking motion is used to execute this blocking technique. The area used to block is the 'palm' of the foot.

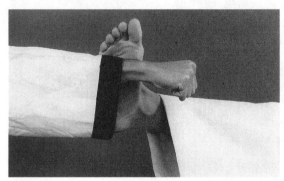

Figure 1

Bal Yup Koom Chi - side heel kick

The area of the foot used for this kick is the heel and part of the foot with the toes pointing slightly downwards.

Figure 2

Bal Ahp Buri Yup - front outer side of the foot

This attack uses the outer edge of the foot just below the small toe, and the kick is executed in the same way as a side snap kick (see page 57). The foot must be pulled backwards towards the ankle when utilising this strike.

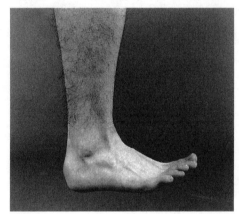

Figure 3

Bal Deung - instep

The contact area in this technique is the top part of the foot just above the big toe to the third toe. The strike is performed in a similar motion to a roundhouse kick.

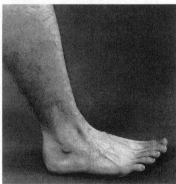

Figure 4

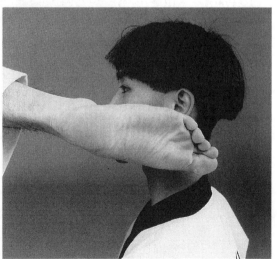

Application

Bal Dwee Koom Chi - heel

This strike uses the rear of the heel where there is a strong bone. The technique requires the body of the attacker to be turned away from the target and is executed using a side kick or back kick.

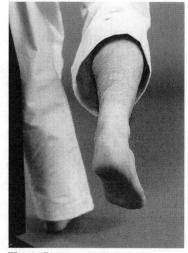

Figure 5

Application

Bal Dwee Koom Chi Yup Ba Dak - side of heel under the foot

This technique uses the outer side of the heel to stamp on an opponent's foot.

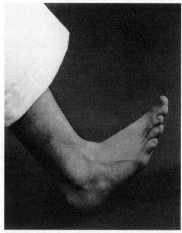

Figure 6

Moo Roop - knee

This attack utilises the top of the knee cap as this is very strong. When the attack is executed, the knee must be bent to give strength to the knee cap when striking an opponent. This attack can either be used to strike the groin area or the face when the opponent's head is pulled downwards (fig. 8).

Figure 7

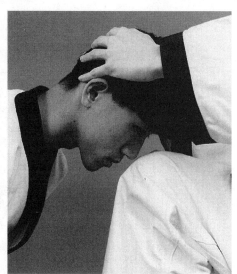

Figure 8

Stances

Joon Bee Jase

Ba Sa Hee Jase

Naihanji Jase

Ship Soo Jase

Kong Sang Koon Jase

Wan Shiew Jase

Dam Twae Jase

Seo Rim Jang Kwon Jase

Dae Ryun Jase

Pyung Lip Jase

Dwee Bal Ja Lip Jase

Bal Moa Sogi Jase

Bal Bul Ri Go Moa Sogi Jase

Pyung Lip Tro Sogi Jase

Chon Gool Jase

Hu Gul Jase

Chwe Ha Dan Jase

Sa Goh Rip Jase

Kee Mahk Jase

Kyo Cha Rip Jase - cross-leg stance

Han Bal Sogi Jase (A)
- one-knee stance

Han Bal Sogi Jase (B)
- crane stance

33

Basic movements

Ha Dan Mahk Kee - low block

From Joon Bee Jase, step forwards with the left leg into a front stance and at the same time pull the left fist to the right shoulder and move the right fist in front of the body. Then simultaneously execute a low block with the left arm while pulling the right fist to the right side. The left arm should be parallel to the left thigh, with the right palm facing upwards at the side of the ribcage. Look forwards.

Figure 1

Figure 2

Figure 3

Application

Sang Dan Mahk Kee - high block

From Joon Bee Jase, step forwards with the left leg into a front stance and bring the left fist to the lower right side while bringing the right fist to the left shoulder. Then simultaneously pull the left arm up to execute a high block while bringing the right fist to the right side. The left fist should be approximately one fist width away from the forehead and the right palm should face upwards at the side of the ribcage. Look forwards.

Figure 4

Figure 5

Figure 6

Application

Bahk Ye Seo Ahn Euro Mahk Kee - outside to inside block

From Joon Bee Jase, step forwards with the left leg into a front stance and bring the left arm to the left side as far as possible. At the same time, bring the right fist to the front of the body. Then simultaneously pull the left arm forwards to execute an outside to inside block while pulling the right fist to the right side. The top of the left fist should be at eye level, with the palm facing towards the body and the right palm facing upwards at the side of the ribcage. Look forwards.

Figure 7

Figure 8

Figure 9

Application

Ahn Ye Seo Bahk Euro Mahk Kee - inside to outside block

From Joon Bee Jase, step forwards with the left leg into a front stance and bring the left arm to the lower right side. At the same time, bring the right fist up to the left shoulder. Then simultaneously execute an inside to outside block with the left arm while pulling the right fist to the right side of the body. The top of the left fist should be at eye level, with the palm facing towards the body and the right palm facing upwards at the side of the ribcage. Look forwards.

Figure 10

Figure 11

Figure 12

Application

Tro Bahk Ye Seo Ahn Euro Mahk Kee - reverse outside to inside middle block

From Joon Bee Jase, step forwards with the left leg into a front stance and bring the left fist in front of the body while bringing the right arm to the right side as far as possible. Then simultaneously execute a reverse right arm outside to inside block while pulling the left fist to the left side. The top of the right fist should be at eye level and the left palm should face upwards at the side of the ribcage. Look forwards.

Figure 13

Figure 14

Figure 15

Application

Tro Ahn Ye Seo Bahk Euro Mahk Kee - reverse inside to outside middle block

From Joon Bee Jase, step forwards with the left leg into a front stance and bring the right fist in front of the body while bringing the left fist to the right shoulder. Then simultaneously execute a reverse right arm inside to outside block while pulling the left fist to the left side. The top of the right fist should be at eye level and the left palm should face upwards at the side of the ribcage. Look forwards.

Figure 16

Figure 17

Figure 18

Application

Sang Soo Ahn Ye Seo Bahk Euro Mahk Kee - double arm middle block

From Joon Bee Jase, step forwards with the left leg into a front stance and bring both fists to the right side of the body. Execute a double arm inside to outside block with the left arm blocking and the right fist supporting the left elbow. The top of the left fist should be at eye level with the right palm facing upwards. Look forwards.

Figure 19

Figure 20

Figure 21

Application

Sang Soo Ha Dan Mahk Kee - double arm low block

From Joon Bee Jase, step forwards with the left leg into a forward stance and bring both fists to the right side of the body in a cross block position. Execute a double low cross block to the front of the body at about waist height. Look forwards.

Figure 22

Figure 23

Figure 24

Application

Hu Gul Yup Mahk Kee - side block back stance

From Joon Bee Jase, step forwards with the left leg into a back stance, and at the same time bring the left fist to the lower right side of the body and the right fist to the left shoulder. Simultaneously execute an inside to outside single arm block with the left arm while pulling the right fist as far back to the right side of the body as possible. The top of the left fist should be at eye level and the right palm should face upwards at the side of the ribcage. The body should turn 90° and the right fist should not be seen when viewed from the front. Look forwards.

Figure 25

Figure 26

Figure 27

Application

Hu Gul Ha Dan Mahk Kee - low block back stance

From Joon Bee Jase, step forwards with the left leg into a back stance, and at the same time bring the left fist to the right shoulder while the right fist moves in front of the body. Simultaneously execute a single arm low block with the left arm while pulling the right fist as far back to the right side of the body as possible. The left arm should be parallel to the left thigh and the right palm should face upwards at the side of the ribcage. The body should turn 90° and the right fist should not be seen when viewed from the front. Look forwards.

Figure 28

Figure 29

Figure 30

Application

Hu Gul Sang Dan Mahk Kee - high block back stance

From Joon Bee Jase, step forwards with the left leg into a back stance, and at the same time bring the left fist to the lower right side of the body and bring the right fist to the left shoulder. Simultaneously execute a single arm high block with the left arm while pulling the right fist as far back to the right side of the body as possible. The left fist should be about one fist width away from the forehead and the right palm should face upwards at the side of the ribcage. The body should turn 90° and the right fist should not be seen when viewed from the front. Look forwards.

Figure 31

Figure 32

Figure 33

Application

Hu Gul Sang Soo Ha Dan Mahk Kee - double arm low block back stance

From Joon Bee Jase, step forwards with the left leg into a back stance, and at the same time bring the left fist to the right shoulder and the right fist to the right side of the body. Execute a double arm low block. The left arm should be parallel to the left thigh, with the right forearm below the solar plexus, palm facing upwards. Look forwards.

Figure 34

Figure 35

Figure 36

Application

41

Sang Soo Soo Do Joong Dan Mahk Kee - double knife hand middle block

From Joon Bee Jase, step forwards with the left leg into a back stance and bring both open hands to the right side of the body. Execute a double knife hand middle block with the left fingertips at eye level and the palm facing downwards. The right palm should face upwards below the solar plexus. Look forwards.

Figure 37   Figure 38

Figure 39

Sang Soo Soo Do Sang Dan Mahk Kee - double knife hand high block back stance

From Joon Bee Jase, step forwards with the left leg into a back stance and bring both open hands to the right side of the body. Execute a double knife hand high block with the left wrist at eye level and the palm facing downwards. The right palm should face upwards below the solar plexus. Look forwards.

Figure 40   Figure 41

Figure 42   Application

Sang Soo Soo Do Ha Dan Mahk Kee - double knife hand low block back stance

From Joon Bee Jase, step forwards with the left leg into a back stance and bring the left open hand to the right shoulder and the right open hand to the right side of the body. Execute a double knife hand low block with the left arm parallel to the left thigh and the palm facing downwards. The right palm should face upwards below the solar plexus. Look forwards.

Figure 43   Figure 44

Figure 45   Application

Sang Soo Ahn Ye Seo Bahk Euro Mahk Kee - double inside to outside block back stance

From Joon Bee Jase, step forwards with the left leg into a back stance and bring both fists to the right side of the body. Execute a double arm inside to outside block with the top of the left fist at eye level and the left palm facing towards the body. The right fist should support the left arm with the right forearm in front of the body. Look forwards.

Figure 46   Figure 47

Figure 48   Application

Hu Gul Bahk Ye Seo Anh Euro Mahk Kee - outside to inside block back stance

From Joon Bee Jase, step forwards with the left leg into a back stance and bring both fists to the left side of the body. Execute a left arm outside to inside block with the top of the left fist at eye level and the left palm facing towards the body. The right fist should be pulled to the right side of the body with the palm facing upwards at the side of the ribcage. Look forwards.

Figure 49   Figure 50

Figure 51

Application

Han Son Hu Gul Bahk Ye Seo Ahn Euro Mahk Kee (A) - outside to inside palm block

From Joon Bee Jase, step forwards with the left leg into a back stance and bring the left open hand and the right fist to the left side of the body. Execute a left arm outside to inside palm block with the top of the left fingertips at eye level. The right fist should be pulled to the right side of the body with the palm facing upwards at the side of the ribcage. Look forwards.

Figure 52

Figure 53

Figure 54

Application

Chwe Ha Dan Soo Do Mahk Kee - ground block knife hand

From Joon Bee Jase, step forwards with the left leg into a very long and low stance and bring both open hands to the right side of the body. Execute a left arm low knife hand ground block with the left arm parallel to the left thigh and the right open hand below the solar plexus, palm facing upwards. Look forwards.

Figure 55

Figure 56

Figure 57

Application

Bal Ja Ba Mahk Kee - defence by holding the leg

From Joon Bee Jase, step the left foot in front of and over the right foot into a cross foot stance, bend the knees and bring both open hands to the sides of the body. Execute a double arm palm block to protect the lower section of the body with both wrists facing each other. Look forwards.

Figure 58

Figure 59

Figure 60

Application

Yuk Soo Do Mahk Kee - ridge/knife hand block

From Joon Bee Jase, step forwards with the left leg into a stance slightly wider than shoulder width, with both knees straight, and bring the left open hand to the left side and the right open hand to the right side. Simultaneously execute a reverse knife hand block with the right palm while bringing the left hand to the rear of the left side. Look forwards.

Figure 61

Application

Joong Dan Kong Kyuk - middle punch front stance

From Joon Bee Jase, step forwards with the left leg into a front stance and bring the left fist to the left side and the right arm in front of the solar plexus. Simultaneously execute a left arm middle punch and bring the right fist to the right side of the ribcage with the palm facing upwards. Look forwards.

Figure 62

Figure 63

Figure 64

47

Sang Dan Kong Kyuk - high punch front stance

From Joon Bee Jase, step forwards with the left leg into a front stance and bring the left fist to the left side and the right arm below the solar plexus. Simultaneously execute a left arm high punch and bring the right fist to the right side of the ribcage with the palm facing upwards. Look forwards.

Figure 65   Figure 66   Figure 67

Kwan Soo Kong Kyuk - spear hand attack

From Joon Bee Jase, step forwards with the left leg into a front stance and block down with the right open hand while pulling the left knife hand to the left side of the body. Execute a left arm knife hand attack. The right open hand should remain in the same position just underneath the left elbow. Look forwards.

Figure 68

Figure 69   Figure 70

48

Kwan Soo Tro Kong Kyuk - reverse spear hand attack

From Joon Bee Jase, step forwards with the left leg into a front stance and block down with the left open hand while pulling the right knife hand to the right side. Execute a reverse right arm knife hand attack. The left open hand should remain in the same position just underneath the left elbow. Look forwards.

Figure 71

Figure 72

Figure 73

Application

Pal Koop Kong Kyuk/Chi Kee - elbow attack

From Joon Bee Jase, step forwards with the left leg into a front stance and bring the left fist to the left side while bringing the right open hand to the front of the body. Execute an elbow attack to the right palm with the left elbow. The arm should be at the same height as the solar plexus. Look forwards.

Figure 74

Figure 75

Figure 76

49

Tro Pal Koop Kong/Kyuk Chi Kee - reverse elbow attack

From Joon Bee Jase, step forwards with the left leg into a front stance and bring the right fist to the right side while bringing the left open hand to the front of the body. Execute an elbow attack to the left palm with the right elbow. The arm should be at the same height as the solar plexus. Look forwards.

Figure 77

Figure 78

Figure 79

Application

Tro Joong Dan Kong Kyuk - reverse middle punch

From Joon Bee Jase, step forwards with the left leg into a front stance and bring the right fist to the right side and the left fist to the front of the body. Simultaneously execute a reverse middle punch with the right arm while bringing the left fist to the left side. The left palm should face upwards at the side of the ribcage. Look forwards.

Figure 80

Figure 81

Figure 82

Application

Tro Sang Dan Kong Kyuk - reverse high punch

From Joon Bee Jase, step forwards with the left leg into a front stance and bring the right fist to the right side and the left fist to the front of the body. Simultaneously execute a reverse high punch with the right arm while bringing the left fist to the left side. The left palm should face upwards at the side of the ribcage. Look forwards.

Figure 83

Figure 84

Figure 85

Application

Sang Dan Soo Do Kong Kyuk - high knife hand attack

From Joon Bee Jase, step forwards with the left leg into a front stance and bring the right open hand to the right side and the left fist to the front of the body. Execute a high right arm knife hand attack and bring the left fist to the left side of the body. The right palm should face upwards with the left palm facing upwards at the side of the ribcage. Look forwards.

Figure 86   Figure 87

Figure 88   Application

Pal Koop Kong Kyuk/Chi Kee - elbow attack

From Joon Bee Jase, step forwards with the left leg into a horse stance and bring both fists to the right side of the body. Execute an elbow attack with the left elbow. The right palm should face upwards at the side of the ribcage. Look forwards.

Figure 89   Figure 90

Figure 91

Application

Yuk Jin Kong Kyuk - reverse punch

From Joon Bee Jase, step forwards with the left leg into a back stance and execute a left arm knife hand attack while pulling the right fist to the right side. Execute a right arm middle punch and pull the left fist to the left side. The left palm should face upwards at the side of the ribcage. Look forwards.

Figure 92

Figure 93

Figure 94

Hoeng Jin Kong Kyuk - side punch

From Joon Bee Jase, step forwards with the left leg into horse stance and bring the left fist to the left side and the right fist in front of the body. Execute a side punch with the left arm and pull the right fist to the right side of the body. The right palm should face upwards at the side of the ribcage. Look towards the left fist.

Figure 95   Figure 96

Figure 97   Application

Kicking techniques

Bal Ap Podo Oll Lee Kee (Ap Cha Kee) - front straight up stretching kick

From Joon Bee Jase, shift weight to the right leg and execute a straight leg raising kick with the left leg, looking up towards the left foot.

Figure 1

Figure 2

Figure 3

Bal Yup Podo Oll Lee Kee (Yuk Cha Kee) - side straight up stretching kick

From Joon Bee Jase, shift weight to the right leg and execute a straight side leg raising kick with the left leg. The body should be sideways on to the target. Look up towards the left foot.

Figure 4

Figure 5

Figure 6

Bahk Ye Seo Ahn Euro Cha Kee - outside to inside kick

From Joon Bee Jase, shift weight to the right leg and swing the left leg upwards (with the knee straight) at approximately 30° to the outside of the body; bring the foot directly above and in front of the body and then pull the leg straight down the centre. The heel of the kicking foot must be pulled back ready to strike. Look up towards the left foot.

Figure 7

Figure 8

Figure 9

Application

Ahn Ye Seo Bahk Euro Cha Kee - inside to outside kick

From Joon Bee Jase, shift weight to the right leg and swing the left leg upwards (with the knee straight) at approximately 30° to the inside of the body; bring the foot directly above and in front of the body and then pull the leg straight down the centre. The heel of the kicking foot must be pulled back ready to strike. Look up towards the left foot.

Figure 10

Figure 11

Figure 12

Ap Cha Nut Kee (Ap Podo Cha Kee) - front snap kick

From Joon Bee Jase, shift weight to the right leg and lift the left knee to about chest height. Execute a front snap kick with the left leg and simultaneously thrust hips forwards to increase the distance and power of the kick, looking up towards the left foot.

Figure 13   Figure 14   Figure 15

Yuk Cha Kee (Yuk Podo Cha Kee) - side snap kick

From Joon Bee Jase, shift weight to the right leg and lift the left knee up to about waist height with the body sideways on to the target. Fully extend the left leg and execute a side snap kick, looking up towards the left foot.

Figure 16   Figure 17

Figure 18   Application

Peet Cha Kee - reverse round house kick

From Joon Bee Jase, shift weight to the right leg and lift the left knee up to about waist height with the body sideways on to the target. Extend the left leg while raising and twisting the left foot outwards from the body to execute a reverse round house kick, looking up towards the left foot.

Figure 19

Figure 20

Figure 21

Dull Ryo Cha Kee - round house kick

From Joon Bee Jase, shift weight to the right leg and lift the left knee up to about waist height. Fully extend the left leg, simultaneously twisting the left foot inwards to execute a round house kick. The body should be sideways on to the target on impact. Look up towards the left foot.

Figure 22

Figure 23

Figure 24

Dwi Podo Cha Kee - back snap kick

From Joon Bee Jase, shift weight to the right leg and turn the body to face away from the target. Lift the left knee up to about waist height and then fully extend the left leg while twisting the left foot to execute a back snap kick. The left foot should point downwards with the body leaning forwards and away from the target. Look up towards the left foot.

Figure 25   Figure 26   Figure 27

Moo Roop Cha Kee - knee attack

From Joon Bee Jase, shift weight to the left leg, lift the right knee upwards to chest height and execute a knee attack. The body should be bent forwards. Look forwards.

Figure 28   Figure 29

Figure 30   Application

Chit Bal Kee - stamping kick

From Joon Bee Jase, shift weight to the right leg, lift the left foot to the right knee and shift the left leg out and downwards into a horse stance to complete a left leg stamping kick.

Figure 31

Figure 32

Figure 33

Dwi Dull Ryo Cha Kee - back spinning kick

From Joon Bee Jase, shift weight to the right leg and turn the body to face away from the target. Turn to the left, raise the left leg and straighten the knee while pulling the left foot back to push the left heel forwards. With the knee straightened all the way, execute a spinning back kick with the left leg, looking up towards the left foot.

Figure 34

Figure 35

Figure 36

Dwi Cha Kee - heel kick

From Joon Bee Jase, shift weight to the right leg with the body facing away from the target and looking over the left shoulder. Lift the left heel to the rear of the body but keep the left knee bent to execute a heel kick, looking towards the rear of the body.

Figure 37

Figure 38

Figure 39

Overview of Hyungs

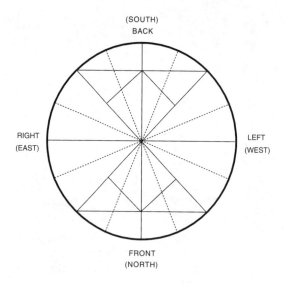

KEE CHO HYUNG

PYUNG AHN CHO DAN

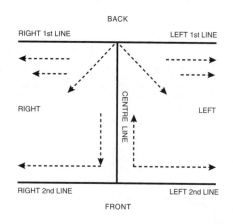

PYUNG AHN EE DAN

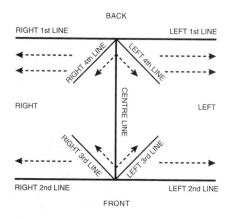

PYUNG AHN SAM DAN

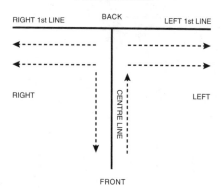

PYUNG AHN SA DAN

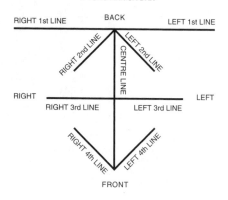

PYUNG AHN OH DAN

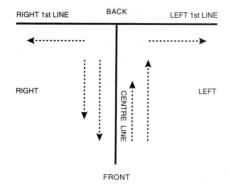

BASSA HEE

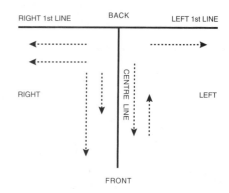

CHIL SUNG IL RO

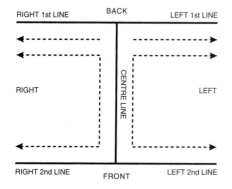

CHIL SUNG EE RO

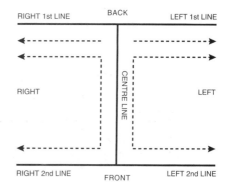

CHIL SUNG SAM RO

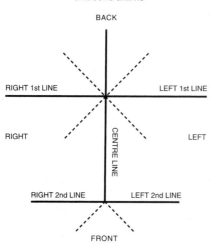

NAIHANJI CHO DAN

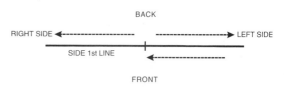

continued

NAIHANJI EE DAN

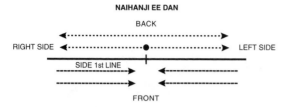

NAIHANJI SAM DAN

SHIP SOO

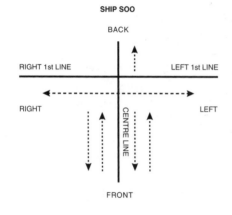

JIN DO

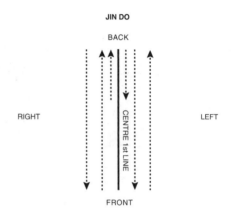

KONG SANG GOON

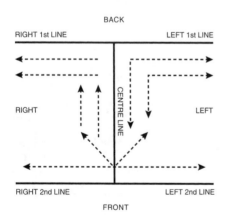

ROHAI

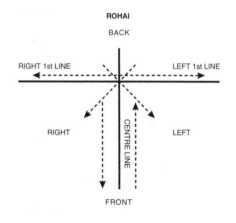

Kee Cho Hyung

Kee Cho Hyung is structured so that beginners can practise basic techniques as a coherent linked exercise:

Kee Cho Hyung Il Boo

Kee Cho Hyung Ee Boo

Kee Cho Hyung Sam Boo.

Kee Cho Hyung Direction

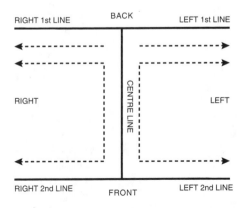

Kee Cho Hyung Il Boo

Basic form I (20 movements)

Joon Bee Jase
Ready stance.

❶ *Ha Dan Mahk Kee*
Look to the left and turn 90° onto the first left line, left foot forwards. Execute a low block with the left arm in front stance.

❷ *Joong Dan Kong Kyuk*
Step forwards with the right foot and middle punch with the right fist in front stance.

❸ *Ha Dan Mahk Kee*
Look to the right and turn 180° onto the first right line, right foot forwards. Execute a low block with the right arm in front stance.

❹ *Joong Dan Kong Kyuk*
Step forwards with the left foot and middle punch with the left fist in front stance.

❺ *Ha Dan Mahk Kee*
Look to the left and turn 90° onto the centre line, left foot forwards. Execute a low block with the left arm in front stance.

❻ *Joong Dan Kong Kyuk* Step forwards with the right foot and middle punch with the right fist in front stance.

❼ *Joong Dan Kong Kyuk* Step forwards with the left foot and middle punch with the left fist in front stance.

❽ *Joong Dan Kong Kyuk [Ki-ahp]* Step forwards with the right foot, execute a middle punch with the right fist in front stance and **shout.**

❾ *Ha Dan Mahk Kee* Look to the left, move the left foot and turn 270° onto the second right line, left foot forwards. Execute a low block with the left arm in front stance.

❿ *Joong Dan Kong Kyuk* Step forwards with the right foot and middle punch with the right fist in front stance.

⓫ *Ha Dan Mahk Kee* Look to the right and turn 180° onto the second left line, right foot forwards. Execute a low block with the right arm in front stance.

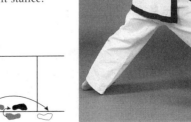

⓬ *Joong Dan Kong Kyuk*
Step forwards with the left foot and middle punch with the left fist in front stance.

⓭ *Ha Dan Mahk Kee*
Look to the left and turn 90° onto the centre line, left foot forwards. Execute a low block with the left arm in front stance.

⓮ *Joong Dan Kong Kyuk*
Step forwards with the right foot and middle punch with the right fist in front stance.

⓯ *Joong Dan Kong Kyuk*
Step forwards with the left foot and middle punch with the left fist in front stance.

⓰ *Joong Dan Kong Kyuk* [Ki-ahp]
Step forwards with the right foot, execute a middle punch with the right fist in front stance and **shout.**

⓱ *Ha Dan Mahk Kee*
Look to the left, move the left foot and turn 270° onto the first left line, left foot forwards. Execute a low block with the left arm in front stance.

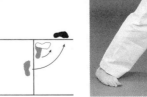

⓲ *Joong Dan Kong Kyuk* Step forwards with the right foot and middle punch with the right fist in front stance.

⓳ *Ha Dan Mahk Kee* Look to the right and turn 180° onto the first right line, right foot forwards. Execute a low block with the right arm in front stance.

⓴ *Joong Dan Kong Kyuk* Step forwards with the left foot and middle punch with the left fist in front stance.

Ba-ro Jase Pull the left foot back into return stance.

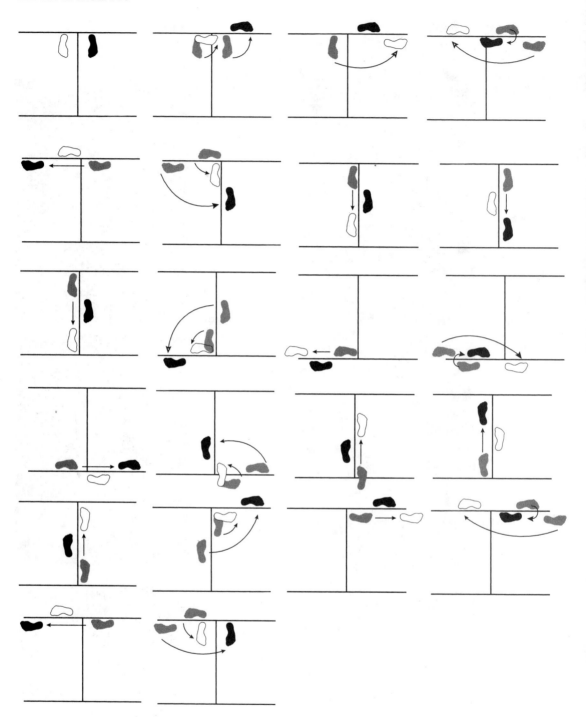

Kee Cho Hyung Ee Boo

Basic form II (20 movements)

Joon Bee Jase
Ready stance.

❶ *Ha Dan Mahk Kee*
Look to the left and turn 90° onto the first left line, left foot forwards. Execute a low block with the left arm in front stance.

❷ *Sang Dan Kong Kyuk*
Step forwards with the right foot and high punch with the right arm in front stance.

❸ *Ha Dan Mahk Kee*
Look to the right and turn 180° onto the first right line, right foot forwards. Execute a low block with the right arm in front stance.

❹ *Sang Dan Kong Kyuk*
Step forwards with the left foot and high punch with the left fist in front stance.

❺ *Ha Dan Mahk Kee*
Look to the left and turn 90° onto the centre line, left foot forwards. Execute a low block with the left arm in front stance.

❻ *Sang Dan Mahk Kee*
Step forwards with the right foot and high block with the right arm in front stance.

❼ *Sang Dan Mahk Kee*
Step forwards with the left foot and high block with the left arm in front stance.

❽ *Sang Dan Mahk Kee [Ki-ahp]*
Step forwards with the right foot, execute a high block with the right arm in front stance and **shout.**

❾ *Ha Dan Mahk Kee*
Look to the left, move the left foot and turn 270° onto the second right line, left foot forwards. Low block with the left arm in front stance.

❿ *Sang Dan Kong Kyuk*
Step forwards with the right foot and high punch with the right fist in front stance.

⓫ *Ha Dan Mahk Kee*
Look to the right and turn 180° onto the second left line, right foot forwards. Execute a low block with the right arm in front stance.

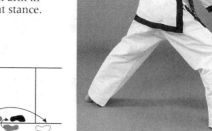

⓬ *Sang Dan Kong Kyuk*
Step forwards with the left foot and high punch with the left fist in front stance.

⓭ *Ha Dan Mahk Kee*
Look to the left and turn 90° onto the centre line, left foot forwards. Execute a low block with the left arm in front stance.

⓮ *Sang Dan Mahk Kee*
Step forwards with the right foot and high block with the right arm in front stance.

⓯ *Sang Dan Mahk Kee*
Step forwards with the left foot and high block with the left arm in front stance.

⓰ *Sang Dan Mahk Kee [Ki-ahp]*
Step forwards with the right foot, execute a high block with the right arm in front stance and **shout.**

⓱ *Ha Dan Mahk Kee*
Look to the left, move the left foot and turn 270° onto the first left line, left foot forwards. Execute a low block with the left arm in front stance.

⑱ *Sang Dan Kong Kyuk*
Step forwards with the right foot and high punch with the right fist in front stance.

⑲ *Ha Dan Mahk Kee*
Look to the right and turn 180° onto the first right line, right foot forwards. Execute a low block with the right arm in front stance.

⑳ *Sang Dan Kong Kyuk*
Step forwards with the left foot and high punch with the left fist in front stance.

Ba-ro Jase
Pull the left foot back into return stance.

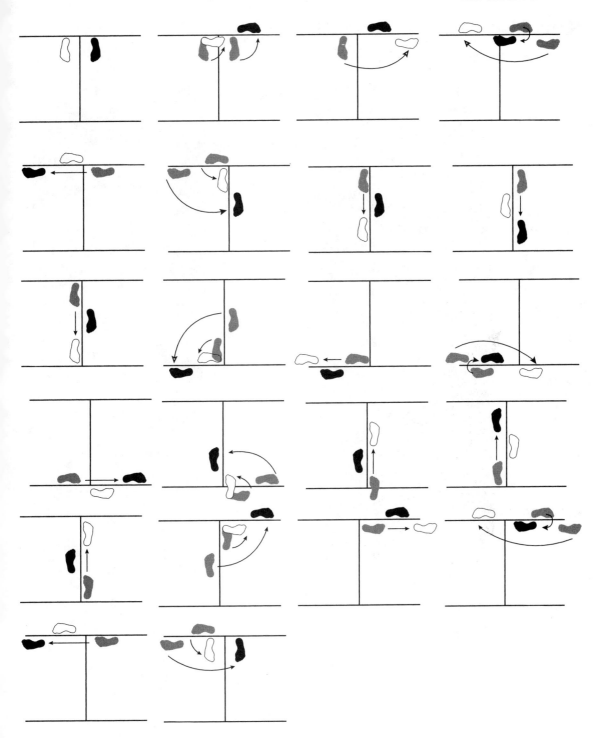

Kee Cho Hyung Sam Boo

Basic form III (20 movements)

Joon Bee Jase
Ready stance.

❶ *Joong Dan Mahk Kee*
Look to the left and turn 90° onto the first left line, left foot forwards. Execute a middle block with the left arm in back stance.

❷ *Joong Dan Kong Kyuk*
Step forwards with the right foot and middle punch with the right fist in front stance.

❸ *Joong Dan Mahk Kee*
Look to the right and turn 180° onto the first right line, right foot forwards. Execute a middle block with the right arm in back stance.

❹ *Joong Dan Kong Kyuk*
Step forwards with the left foot and middle punch with the left fist in front stance.

❺ *Ha Dan Mahk Kee*
Look to the left and turn 90° onto the centre line, left foot forwards. Execute a low block with the left arm in front stance.

❻ *Hoeng Jin Kong Kyuk*
Step forwards with the right foot and side punch with the right fist in horse stance.

❼ *Hoeng Jin Kong Kyuk*
Step forwards with the left foot and side punch with the left fist in horse stance.

❽ *Hoeng Jin Kong Kyuk [Ki-ahp]*
Step forwards with the right foot, execute a side punch with the right fist in horse stance and **shout.**

❾ *Joong Dan Mahk Kee*
Look to the left, move the left foot and turn 270° onto the second right line, left foot forwards. Execute a middle block with the left arm in back stance.

❿ *Joong Dan Kong Kyuk*
Step forwards with the right foot and middle punch with the right fist in front stance.

⓫ *Joong Dan Mahk Kee*
Look to the right and turn 180° onto the second left line, right foot forwards. Execute a middle block with the right arm in back stance.

⓬ *Joong Dan Kong Kyuk* Step forwards with the left foot and middle punch with the left fist in front stance.

⓭ *Ha Dan Mahk Kee* Look to the left and turn 90° onto the centre line, left foot forwards. Execute a low block with the left arm in front stance.

⓮ *Hoeng Jin Kong Kyuk* Step forwards with the right foot and side punch with the right fist in horse stance.

⓯ *Hoeng Jin Kong Kyuk* Step forwards with the left foot and side punch with the left fist in horse stance.

⓰ *Hoeng Jin Kong Kyuk [Ki-ahp]* Step forwards with the right foot, execute a side punch with the right fist in horse stance and **shout.**

⓱ *Joong Dan Mahk Kee* Look to the left, move the left foot and turn 270° onto the first left line, left foot forwards. Execute a middle block with the left arm in back stance.

18 *Joong Dan Kong Kyuk*
Step forwards with the right foot and middle punch with the right fist in front stance.

19 *Joong Dan Mahk Kee*
Look to the right and turn 180° onto the first right line, right foot forwards. Execute a middle block with the right arm in back stance.

20 *Joong Dan Kong Kyuk*
Step forwards with the left foot and middle punch with the left fist in front stance.

Ba-ro Jase
Pull the left foot back into return stance.

79

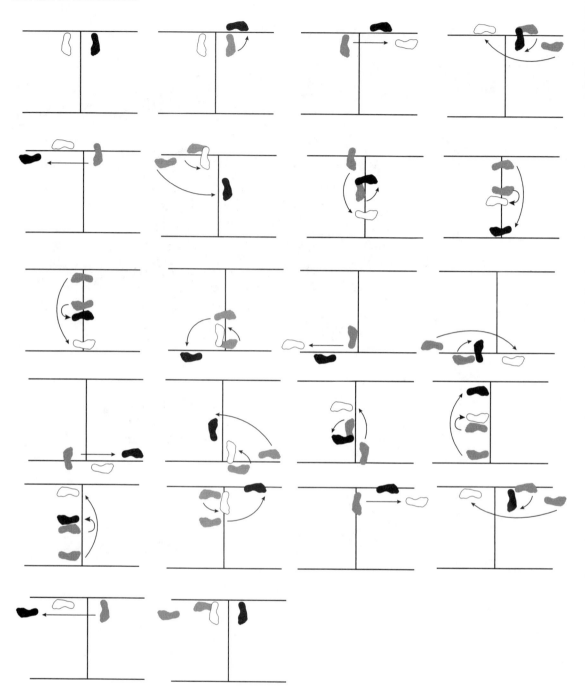

Pyung Ahn Hyung

Pyung Ahn Hyung was originally called Je Nam Hyung. It was devised approximately 130 years ago by separating Je Nam Hyung into five components. Pyung Ahn Hyung symbolises the Turtle.

Pyung Ahn Cho Dan Hyung

Pyung Ahn I (22 movements)

Pyung Ahn Cho Dan Hyung Direction

BACK

RIGHT 1st LINE | LEFT 1st LINE

CENTRE LINE

RIGHT | LEFT

RIGHT 2nd LINE | LEFT 2nd LINE

FRONT

Joon Bee Jase
Ready stance -
looking north.

❶ *Ha Dan Mahk Kee*
Look to the left and turn 90° onto the first left line, left foot forwards. Execute a left hand low block in front stance.

❷ *Joong Dan Kong Kyuk*
Step forwards with the right foot and right hand middle punch in front stance.

❸ *Ha Dan Mahk Kee*
Look to the right and turn 180° onto the first right line, right foot forwards. Execute a right hand low block in front stance.

❹ *Kwon Do Kong Kyuk*
Twist the right fist clockwise, then pull the right foot to 90° to the left and execute a hammer punch by bringing the right fist above the head (movements ❸ and ❹ should be executed in quick succession, applying hip twist).

❺ *Joong Dan Kong Kyuk*
Step forwards with the left foot and left hand middle punch in front stance.

❻ *Ha Dan Mahk Kee*
Look to the left and turn 90° onto the centre line. Execute a left hand low block in front stance.

❼ *Joong Dan Soo Do Mahk Kee*
Immediately execute a left knife hand middle block in front stance (movements **❻** and **❼** should be executed in quick succession, applying hip twist).

❽ *Sang Dan Mahk Kee*
Step forwards with the right foot and execute a right hand high block in front stance.

❾ *Sang Dan Mahk Kee*
Step forwards with the left foot and execute a left hand high block in front stance.

❿ *Sang Dan Mahk Kee [Ki-ahp]*
Step forwards with the right foot, execute a right hand high block in front stance and **shout**.

⓫ *Ha Dan Mahk Kee*
Look to the left, move the left foot and turn 270° onto the second right line, left foot forwards. Execute a left hand low block in front stance.

⓬ *Joong Dan Kong Kyuk*
Step forwards with the right foot and right hand middle punch in front stance.

⓭ *Ha Dan Mahk Kee*
Look to the right and turn 180° onto the second left line, right foot forwards. Execute a right hand low block in front stance.

⓮ *Joong Dan Kong Kyuk*
Step forwards with the left foot and left hand middle punch in front stance.

⓯ *Ha Dan Mahk Kee*
Look to the left and turn 90° onto the centre line, left foot forwards. Execute a left hand low block in front stance.

⓰ *Joong Dan Kong Kyuk*
Step forwards with the right foot and right hand middle punch in front stance.

⓱ *Joong Dan Kong Kyuk*
Step forwards with the left foot and left hand middle punch in front stance.

18 *Joong Dan Kong Kyuk [Ki-ahp]* Step forwards with the right foot, execute a right hand middle punch in front stance and **shout.**

19 *Ha Dan Soo Do Mahk Kee* Look to the left, move the left foot and turn 270° onto the first left line, left foot forwards. Execute a double knife hand low block in back stance.

20 *Ha Dan Soo Do Mahk Kee* Turn 45° to the right, right foot forwards, and execute a double knife hand low block in back stance.

21 *Ha Dan Soo Do Mahk Kee* Turn 135° to the right onto the first right line, right foot forwards. Execute a double knife hand low block in back stance.

22 *Ha Dan Soo Do Mahk Kee* Turn 45° to the left, left foot forwards, and execute a double knife hand low block in back stance.

Ba-ro Jase Pull the left foot back into return stance.

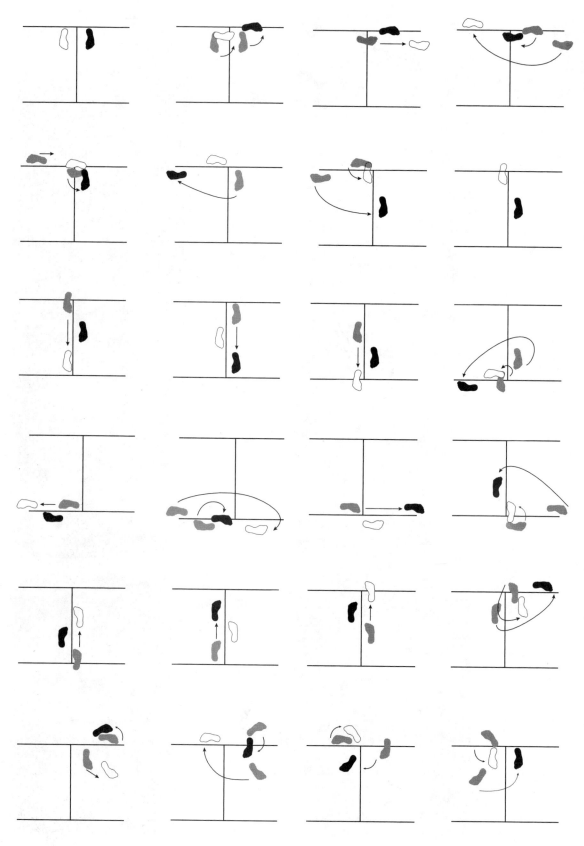

Pyung Ahn Ee Dan Hyung

Pyung Ahn II (29 movements)

Pyung Ahn Ee Dan Hyung Direction

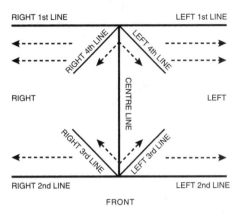

RIGHT 1st LINE   LEFT 1st LINE

RIGHT 4th LINE   LEFT 4th LINE

RIGHT   CENTRE LINE   LEFT

RIGHT 3rd LINE   LEFT 3rd LINE

RIGHT 2nd LINE   LEFT 2nd LINE

FRONT

Joon Bee Jase
Ready stance -
looking north.

❶ *Yang Pal Mahk Kee*
Look to the left and turn 90° onto the first left line, left foot forwards. Execute a left arm middle block with the palm facing north, and a right arm high block in back stance.

❷ *Tu Joo Mok Kong Kyuk/Mahk Kee*
Maintain the same stance and drop the right fist to chest height. Thrust forwards for an upper cut, twisting the hips 90° to the left, left fist above right shoulder in back stance.

❸ *Hoeng Jin Kong Kyuk*
Step forwards with the left foot and side punch with the left hand in horse stance.

❹ *Yang Pal Mahk Kee*
Look to the right and turn 180° onto the first right line, right foot forwards. Execute a right arm middle block with the palm facing north, and a left arm high block in back stance.

87

❺ *Tu Joo Mok Kong Kyuk/Mahk Kee*
Maintain the same stance and drop the left fist to chest height. Thrust forwards for an upper cut, twisting the hips 90° to the right in back stance.

❻ *Hoeng Jin Kong Kyuk*
Step forwards with the right foot and side punch with the right fist in horse stance.

❼ *Prepare stance*
Shift the left foot half a step forwards onto the centre line, then pick up the right foot, holding it against the left knee with both fists on the left side and looking south.

❽ *Yup Podo Cha Kee*
Execute a middle section side kick with the right foot and simultaneously execute a hammer attack with the right fist, then balance on the left leg and bring the right foot to the side of the left leg.

❾ *Sang Soo Joong Dan Soo Do Mahk Kee*
Look to the left and turn 180° onto the centre line, left foot forwards. Execute a double knife hand middle block in back stance.

❿ *Sang Soo Joong Dan Soo Do Mahk Kee*
Step forwards with the right foot and double knife hand middle block in back stance.

⓫ *Sang Soo Joong Dan Soo Do Mahk Kee*
Step forwards with the left foot and double knife hand middle block in back stance.

⓬ *Kwan Soo Kong Kyuk [Ki-ahp]*
Step forwards with the right foot and block with the left arm. Spear hand attack with the right hand in front stance and **shout**.

⓭ *Sang Soo Joong Dan Soo Do Mahk Kee*
Look to the left, move the left foot and turn 270° to the left onto the second right line, left foot forwards. Execute a double knife hand middle block in back stance.

⓮ *Sang Soo Joong Dan Soo Do Mahk Kee*
Look to the right and turn 45° to the right, right foot forwards. Execute a double knife hand middle block in back stance.

⓯ *Sang Soo Joong Dan Soo Do Mahk Kee*
Look to the right and turn 135° to the right onto the second left line, right foot forwards. Execute a double knife hand middle block in back stance.

⓰ *Sang Soo Joong Dan Soo Do Mahk Kee*
Turn 45° to the left, left foot forwards. Execute a double knife hand middle block in back stance.

17 *Tro Ahn Ye Seo Bahk Euro Mahk Kee*
Look to the left and turn 45° to the left onto the centre line, left foot forwards. Execute a reverse inside to outside middle block with the right arm, with the right shoulder pushed forwards slightly, in front stance.

18 *Joong Dan Ap Podo Cha Kee*
Execute a middle front snap kick with the right foot.

19 *Tro Joong Dan Kong Kyuk*
Step forwards with the right foot and reverse middle punch with the left fist, with the left shoulder forwards slightly, in front stance.

20 *Tro Ahn Ye Seo Bahk Euro Mahk Kee*
In the same stance, execute a reverse inside to outside middle block with the left arm.

21 *Joong Dan Ap Podo Cha Kee*
Execute a middle front snap kick with the left foot.

22 *Tro Joong Dan Kong Kyuk*
Step forwards with the left foot and reverse right hand middle punch, with the right shoulder slightly forwards, in front stance.

㉓ *Sang Soo Joong Dan Mahk Kee*
Step forwards with the right foot and double inside to outside middle block in front stance.

㉔ *Ha Dan Mahk Kee*
Look to the left, move the left foot and turn 270° to the left onto the first left line, left foot forwards. Execute a left hand low block in front stance.

㉕ *Han Son Joong Dan Soo Do Mahk Kee*
Maintaining the same stance, immediately execute a left knife hand middle block.

㉖ *Sang Dan Mahk Kee*
Turn 45° to the right and execute a right hand high block in front stance.

㉗ *Ha Dan Mahk Kee*
Look to the right and turn 135° to the right onto the first right line, right foot forwards. Execute a right hand low block in front stance.

㉘ *Han Son Joong Dan Soo Do Mahk Kee*
Maintaining the same stance, immediately execute a right knife hand middle block.

㉙ *Sang Dan Mahk Kee [Ki-ahp]*
Look to the left and turn 45° to the left. Execute a left hand high block in front stance and **shout**.

Ba-ro Jase
Pull the left foot back into return stance.

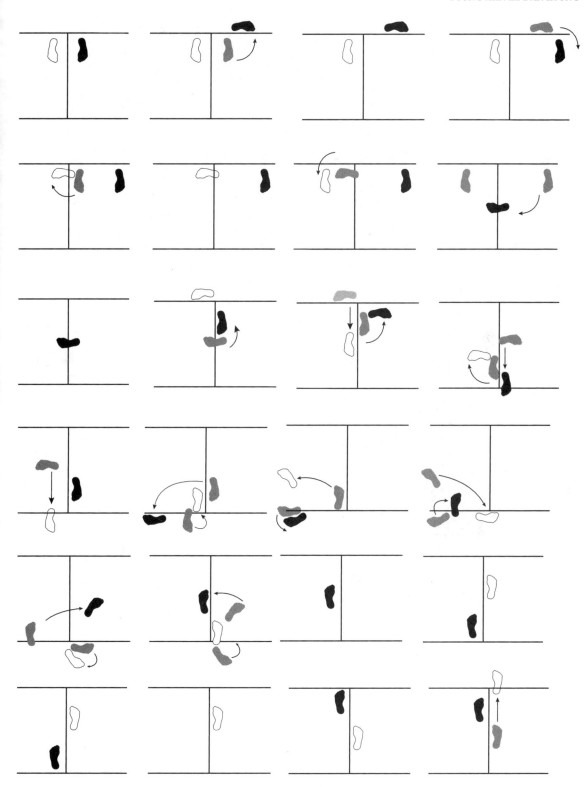

continued

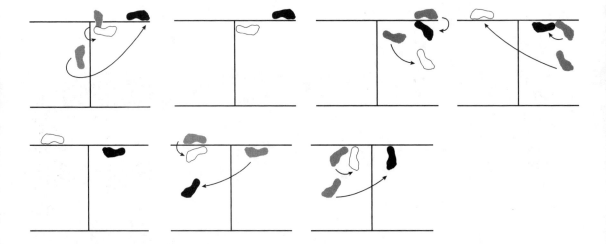

Pyung Ahn Sam Dan Hyung

Pyung Ahn III (27 movements)

Pyung Ahn Sam Dan Hyung Direction

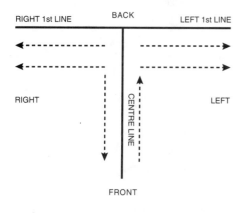

Joon Bee Jase
Ready stance - looking north.

❶ *Joong Dan Yup Mahk Kee*
Look to the left and turn 90° onto the first left line, left foot forwards. Execute a left hand inside to outside middle block in back stance.

❷ Preparation movement
Move the right foot to the side of the left foot so that both feet are together, with the right arm in a low block position and the left arm in a middle block position.

❸ *Ha Dan/Joong Dan Mahk Kee*
Simultaneously execute a low block with the left arm and a middle block with the right arm, keeping both feet together.

❹ *Ha Dan/Joong Dan Mahk Kee*
Simultaneously execute a low block with the right arm and a middle block with the left arm (movements ❸ and ❹ are to be applied in quick succession).

❺ *Joong Dan Yup Mahk Kee* Turn 180° to the right onto the first right line, right foot forwards. Execute a right hand inside to outside middle block in back stance.

❻ Preparation movement Move the left foot to the side of the right foot so that both feet are together and cross both hands, with the left arm in a low block position and the right arm in a middle block position.

❼ *Ha Dan/Joong Dan Mahk Kee* Simultaneously execute a low block with the right arm and a middle block with the left arm.

❽ *Ha Dan/Joong Dan Mahk Kee* Simultaneously execute a low block with the left arm and a middle block with the right arm (movements **❼** and **❽** are to be applied in quick succession).

❾ *Sang Soo Joong Dan Mahk Kee* Look to the left and turn 90° onto the centre line, left foot forwards. Execute a double arm middle block in front stance.

❿ *Kwan Soo Kong Kyuk* Step forwards with the right foot, block with the left arm and immediately execute a knife hand attack with the right hand in front stance.

11 Preparation movement
Bend the right elbow slightly, twist the right hand anti-clockwise and pull it to the right waist. Take a long step towards the north, with the left leg behind the right leg, maintaining forward focus.

12 *Kwon Do Kong Kyuk*
Look to the left, pivot on both feet into horse stance and execute a hammer attack with the left fist.

13 *Joong Dan Kong Kyuk [Ki-ahp]*
Step forwards with the right foot, execute a right hand middle punch in front stance and **shout.**

14 Preparation movement
Move the left foot to the side of the right foot as you pivot on the right foot, turning 180° to the left to face the centre line. Bring both fists to the waist away from the body.

15 *Bahk Ye Seo Ahn Euro Mahk Go Cha Kee*
Execute a right foot outside to inside block kick, and balance on the left leg with the knee bent.

16 *Jit Bal Kee*
Stamp with the right foot into horse stance with both fists at the waist. Twist the body anti-clockwise to prepare for the next move.

97

17 *Kwon Do Kong Kyuk* Hammer attack with the right fist, then quickly pull it back to the right side with the knuckles of both fists on the waist, in horse stance.

18 *Bahk Ye Seo Ahn Euro Mahk Go Cha Kee* Execute a left foot outside to inside block kick, and balance on the right leg with the knee bent.

19 *Jit Bal Kee* Stamp with the left foot into horse stance with both fists at the waist. Twist the body clockwise to prepare for the next move.

20 *Kwon Do Kong Kyuk* Hammer attack with the left fist, then quickly pull it back to the left side of the waist in horse stance.

21 *Bahk Ye Seo Ahn Euro Mahk Go Cha Kee* Execute a right foot outside to inside block kick, and balance on the left leg with the knee bent.

22 *Jit Bal Kee* Stamp with the right foot into horse stance with both fists at the waist. Twist the body anti-clockwise to prepare for the next move.

㉓ *Kwon Do Kong Kyuk*
Hammer attack with the right fist, keeping the left fist at the waist in horse stance.

㉔ *Joong Dan Kong Kyuk*
Step forwards with the left foot and left hand middle punch in front stance.

㉕ Preparation movement
Bring the right foot to the left knee and then stamp it down to the right side into horse stance.

㉖ *Sang Dan Kong Kyuk*
Look to the left and turn 180° to the left onto the first left line. Pivot on the right foot and move the left foot into horse stance. Execute a right arm high punch over the left shoulder and simultaneously execute a left elbow attack to the rear of the body.

㉗ *Sang Dan Kong Kyuk [Ki-ahp]*
Look to the right then jump to the right and execute a left arm high punch over the right shoulder. Simultaneously execute a right elbow attack to back in horse stance and **shout**.

Ba-ro Jase
Pull the right foot back into return stance.

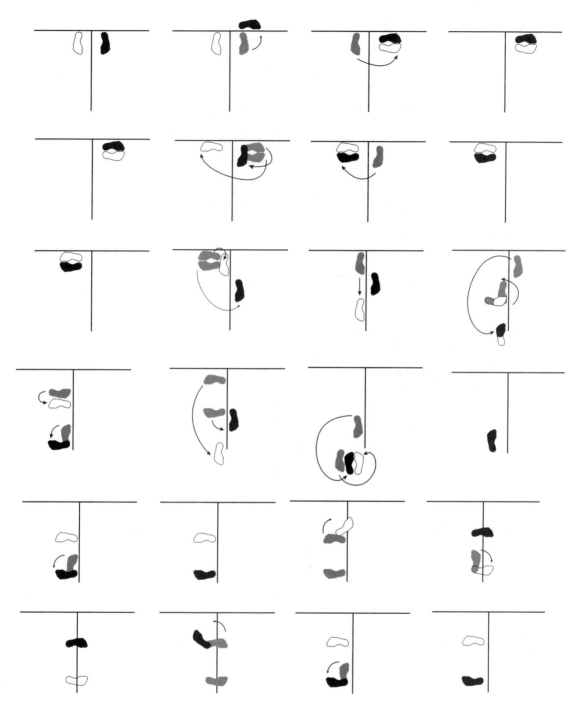

continued

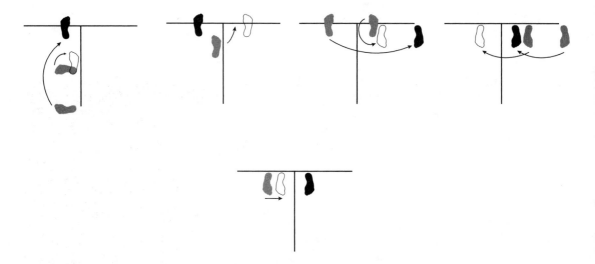

Pyung Ahn Sa Dan Hyung

Pyung Ahn IV (29 movements)

Pyung Ahn Sa Dan Hyung Direction

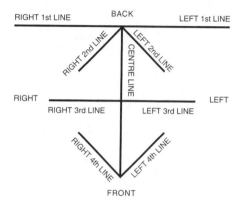

Joon Bee Jase
Ready stance -
looking north.

❶ *Joong Dan/Sang Dan Soo Do Mahk Kee*
Look to the west and turn 90° to the first left line, left foot forwards. Move both hands to the right side and simultaneously execute a left knife hand middle block and right knife hand high block, both palms facing north, in back stance.

❷ *Joong Dan/Sang Dan Soo Do Mahk Kee*
Look to the east and turn 180° to the first right line, right foot forwards. Move both hands to the left side and simultaneously execute a right knife hand middle block and left knife hand high block, both palms facing north, in back stance.

❸ *Sang Soo Ha Dan Mahk Kee*
Look to the north and turn 90° to the centre line, left foot forwards. Drop both hands to the right side of the waist and execute a double hand low X block in front stance.

❹ *Sang Soo Joong Dan Mahk Kee*
Step forwards with the right foot and double arm middle block in back stance.

5 Preparation movement Look 90° to the west, pick up the left foot and hold it beside the right knee. Bring both fists to the right side of the waist.

6 *Yup Podo Cha Kee* Simultaneously execute a side snap kick with the left foot and a left side hammer attack. Pull the left foot back to the right knee and leave the left fist extended.

7 *Pal Koop Kong Kyuk* Step forwards with the left foot and strike the left palm with the right elbow in front stance.

8 Preparation movement Look to the east and turn 180° to the right. Shift the right foot slightly to the right into a back stance and bring both fists to the left side of the waist.

9 Preparation movement Half step forwards with the left foot, bring both hands to the right hip, pick up the right foot and hold it beside the left knee. Bring both fists to the left waist.

10 *Yup Podo Cha Kee* Simultaneously execute a side snap kick with the right foot and a right side hammer attack. Pull the right foot back to the left knee and leave the right fist extended.

⓫ *Pal Koop Kong Kyuk*
Step forwards with the right foot and strike the right palm with the left elbow in front stance.

⓬ *Tro Soo Do Sang Dan Kong Kyuk/Sang Dan Mahk Kee*
Look to the north and turn 90° to the left, pivoting on both feet, left foot forwards. Execute a high left knife hand block and right knife hand high attack.

⓭ *Ap Podo Cha Kee*
High front snap kick with the right foot.

⓮ *Kap Kwon Kong Kyuk [Ki-ahp]*
Jump forwards, landing on the right foot and bring the left foot behind the right foot. Execute a middle back fist attack with the right fist and **shout**.

⓯ Preparation movement
Look to the left and turn 135° to the left, pivoting on the right foot, left foot forwards. Both fists should be at shoulder height, with the arms slightly bent in front stance.

⓰ *Ap Mee Ro Cha Kee*
Simultaneously twist the right fist and execute a right front pushing/snap kick with the right leg, keeping both hands in the same position.

105

17 *Joong Dan Kong Kyuk* Step forwards with the right foot and immediately execute a right arm middle punch in front stance.

18 *Tro Joong Dan Kong Kyuk* Immediately execute a reverse left arm middle punch in front stance.

19 Preparation movement Look to the right and turn 90° to the right, pivoting on the left foot, right foot forwards. Both fists should be at shoulder height with the arms slightly bent in front stance.

20 *Ap Mee Ro Cha Kee* Simultaneously twist the left fist and execute a left front pushing/snap kick, keeping both hands in the same position.

21 *Joong Dan Kong Kyuk* Step forwards with the left foot and immediately execute a left arm middle punch in front stance.

22 *Joong Dan Kong Kyuk* Immediately execute a reverse right hand middle punch.

㉓ *Sang Soo Joong Dan Mahk Kee*
Move the left foot onto the centre line, pivoting on the right foot, left foot forwards. Execute a double arm middle block in back stance.

㉔ *Sang Soo Joong Dan Mahk Kee*
Step forwards with the right foot and double arm middle block in back stance.

㉕ *Sang Soo Joong Dan Mahk Kee*
Step forwards with the left foot and double arm middle block in back stance.

㉖ Preparation movement
Shift the left foot forwards into front stance and bring both open hands at neck height through 45°.

㉗ *Moo Roop Chee Kee [Ki-ahp]*
Execute a right knee attack and pull both hands down either side of the knee with the instep/toes pointing downwards. Balance on the left leg with the left knee bent and **shout.**

㉘ *Sang Soo Joong Dan Soo Do Mahk Kee*
Look to the left and turn 180° to the north, left foot forwards. Execute a double knife hand middle block in back stance (movements ㉗ and ㉘ are to be executed in quick succession).

㉙ *Sang Soo Joong Dan Soo Do Mahk Kee*
Look to the right and turn 45° to the right. Step forwards with the right foot and double knife hand middle block in back stance.

Ba-ro Jase
Look to the north and pull the right foot back into ready stance.

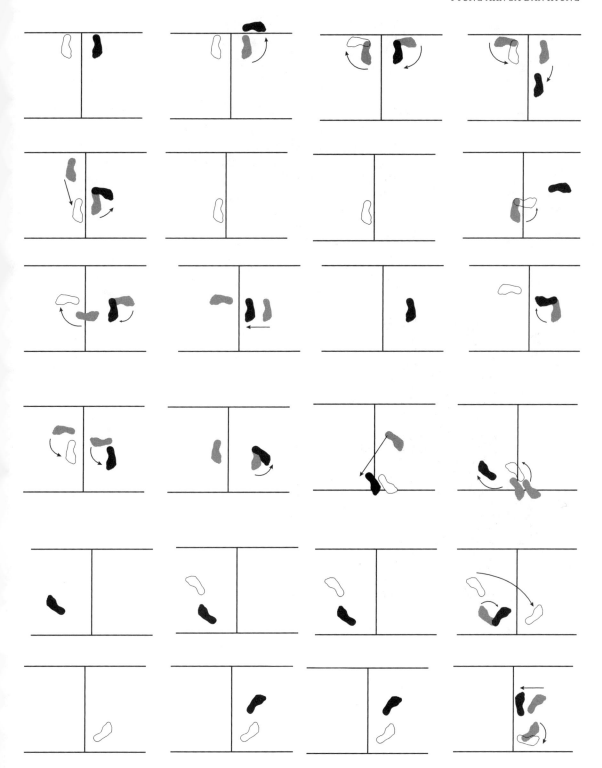

continued

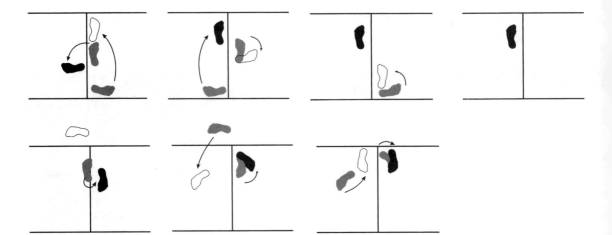

Pyung Ahn Oh Dan Hyung

Pyung Ahn V (29 movements)

Pyung Ahn Oh Dan Hyung Direction

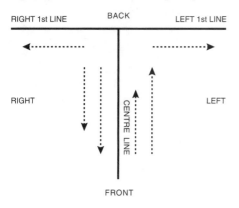

RIGHT 1st LINE   BACK   LEFT 1st LINE

RIGHT   CENTRE LINE   LEFT

FRONT

Joon Bee Jase
Ready stance -
facing north.

❶ *Joong Dan
Yuk Mahk Kee*
Look to the left
and turn 90° to
the west, left
foot forwards.
Execute an
inside to outside
middle block
with the left
arm in back
stance.

❷ *Yuk Jin
Kong Kyuk*
Immediately
execute a
reverse right
arm middle half
punch/block
with the right
elbow slightly
bent in back
stance.

❸ Preparation
movement
Look to the
right and turn
90° to the
north, bringing
the right foot to
the side of the
left foot. Bring
both fists to the
right side of the
waist and apply
hip twist.

❹ *Joong Dan
Yuk Mahk Kee*
Look to the
right and turn
90° to the east,
right foot
forwards.
Execute an
inside to outside
middle block
with the right
arm in back
stance.

❺ *Yuk Jin Kong Kyuk* Immediately execute a reverse left arm middle half punch/block with the left elbow slightly bent in back stance.

❻ Preparation movement Look to the north and turn 90° to the north, bringing the left foot to the side of the right foot. Bring both fists to the left side of the waist and apply hip twist.

❼ *Yang Soo Joong Dan Mahk Kee* Step forwards with the right foot and double arm middle block in front stance.

❽ *Sang Soo Ha Dan Mahk Kee* Bring both fists to the right hip, step forwards with the left foot and execute a low X block in front stance.

❾ *Sang Soo Sang Dan Mahk Kee* Maintaining front stance, pull both fists towards the chest and execute a double knife hand X high block (application: block high level attack).

❿ Preparation movement Rotate both hands and pull them down to the right side of the waist with the left hand in open palm and the right fist clenched.

11 *Soo Do Joong Dan Kong Kyuk*
Execute a left hand knife attack (left hand could be grabbing a stick/hand).

12 *Joong Dan Kong Kyuk [Ki-ahp]*
Step forwards with the right foot, execute a right hand middle punch in front stance and shout.

13 *Bal Ba Dahk Euro Mahk Kee*
Look to the left and turn 180° to the south. Execute an outside to inside block kick with the right foot.

14 Preparation movement
Balance on the left leg with both arms crossed in front of the body, ready for the next movement and facing south.

15 *Ha Dan Mahk Kee*
Step down with the right foot into a horse stance and execute a right arm low block.

16 Preparation movement
Maintaining horse stance, turn 180° to the north, bringing the left hand to the right hip and the right fist to the left shoulder. Extend the left open hand straight out towards the north with open palm.

17 *Bal Ba Dahk Euro Mahk Kee* Execute a right foot outside to inside block kick, striking the left open hand, then hold the foot out, balancing on the left leg with the knee bent.

18 *Pal Koop Kong Kyuk* Stamp down with the right foot into horse stance and immediately execute a right elbow attack.

19 *Sang Soo Joong Dan Mahk Kee* Look to the north, shift the left foot behind the right foot and execute a middle double forearm block.

20 Preparation movement Turn 180° to the south and straighten the right arm while the left arm remains in the same position. Shift the left foot forwards with both knees straight.

21 Jump Push off both feet, jump and twist the body 180° to face east.

22 *Sang Soo Ha Dan Mahk Kee* Land with the right foot in front of the left, half squatting down, and execute a low double fist X block while keeping the back straight.

114

㉓ *Yang Soo Joong Dan Mahk Kee*
Look to the right and turn 90° to the south, right foot forwards. Execute a double arm middle block in front stance.

㉔ *Ha Dan Kwan Soo Kong Kyuk*
Look to the left and turn 180° to the left. Shift the left foot into front stance and execute a low spear hand attack with the right palm at 45° while executing a left fist attack over the right shoulder.

㉕ *Sang Dan/Ha Dan Mahk Kee*
Pull the left foot back into back stance and execute a high 90° block with right arm and a low block with left arm in back stance.

㉖ Preparation movement
Pull the left foot to the side of the right foot, straighten both knees, move the right hip forwards and then twist back into the original position.

㉗ *Sang Soo Sang Dan Mahk Kee*
Face to the north and maintain this focus. Pivot 180° to the left on both feet into a crossed foot stance, with the left foot in front of the right foot, both hands executing a high double arm side block while turning.

㉘ *Ha Dan Kwan Soo Kong Kyuk*
Turn 90° to the right, step forwards with the right foot into front stance and execute a low spear hand attack with the left palm at 45° while executing a right fist attack over the left shoulder.

㉙ *Sang Dan/Ha Dan Mahk Kee*
[Ki-ahp]
Pull the right foot back into
back stance, execute a right
hand low block and a left
hand high block and **shout.**

Ba-ro Jase
Pull the right
foot back into
ready stance.

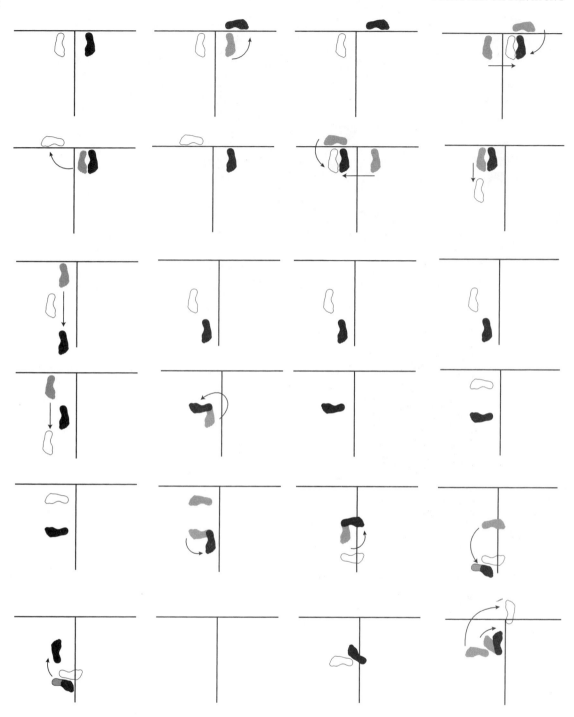

continued

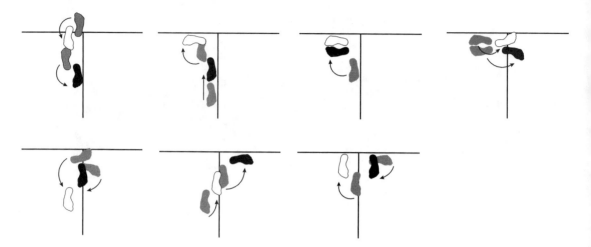

Ba Sa Hee Hyung

Ba Sa Hee Hyung was devised approximately 450 years ago. It is based on the art of boxing and has undergone many changes while evolving into its present form. It was practised by the Buddhist monks at the So Lim Sa temple situated in the Ha Nam region of China, and consists of carefully selected moves from the So Lim Sa techniques, which are executed with the effective use of force and speed. The name of the originator is not known.
Ba Sa Hee Hyung symbolises the Cobra.

Ba Sa Hee Hyung Direction

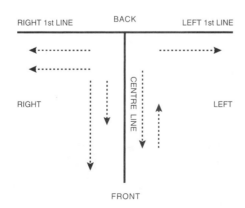

Ba Sa Hee Hyung

(52 movements)

Ba Sa Hee Joon Bee Jase
Ready stance - facing north. Clench the right fist with the left hand, both feet together.

❶ *Ahn Ye Seo Bahk Euro Mahk Kee*
Turn the body 90° to the west whilst facing north, then drop forwards to the north into a crossed foot stance (right in front of left) and execute an inside to outside block with the right arm, with the left hand pressed against the right wrist.

❷ *Ahn Ye Seo Bahk Euro Mahk Kee*
Look to the left and turn 180° to the left to face south. Immediately execute an inside to outside block with the left arm, with the left foot forwards in front stance.

❸ *Tro Ahn Ye Seo Bahk Euro Mahk Kee*
Maintaining the same stance, immediately execute a right arm reverse inside to outside block (movements **❷** and **❸** are to be executed in quick succession).

❹ *Tro Bahk Ye Seo Ahn Euro Mahk Kee*
Look to the right and turn 180° to the right to face north, with the right foot forwards. Execute a reverse left arm outside to inside block in front stance.

❺ *Ahn Ye Seo Bahk Euro Mahk Kee*
Maintaining the same stance, immediately execute an inside to outside block with the right arm (movements **❹** and **❺** are to be executed in quick succession).

❻ *Ha Dan Mahk Kee*
Look to the right, pick up the right foot and hunch the body forwards. At the same time, execute a right hand low block down the side of the right leg whilst looking east.

7 *Bahk Ye Seo Ahn Euro Mahk Kee*
Turn 90° to the right to face east, step forwards into a narrow right leg front stance and execute an outside to inside block with the right arm.

8 *Ahn Ye Seo Bahk Euro Mahk Kee*
Maintaining the same stance, immediately execute a reverse inside to outside block with the left arm (movements **7** and **8** are to be executed in quick succession).

9 Preparation movement
Turn 90° to face north and pivot on both feet into horse stance while bringing both fists to the right side.

10 *Soo Do Kong Kyuk*
Maintaining the same horse stance, immediately execute a knife hand attack with the left hand (movements **10** to **14** are to be executed in quick succession).

11 *Joong Dan Kong Kyuk*
Maintaining the same stance, execute a middle punch with the right fist.

12 *Ahn Ye Seo Bahk Euro Mahk Kee*
Pivot to the left into front stance and execute an inside to outside middle block with the right arm.

⓭ *Joong Dan
Kong Kyuk*
Execute a
middle punch
with the left fist
and move both
feet back into
horse stance.

⓮ *Ahn Ye Seo
Bahk Euro Mahk
Kee*
Pivot to the
right into front
stance and
execute an
inside to outside
middle block
with the left
arm.

⓯ *Sang Soo Soo
Do Joong Dan
Mahk Kee*
Half step with
the left foot
towards the
right foot, and
then step
forwards with
the right foot
into back stance
and execute a
double knife
hand middle
block.

⓰ *Sang Soo Soo
Do Joong Dan
Mahk Kee*
Step forwards
with the left
foot and
execute a
double knife
hand middle
block in back
stance.

⓱ *Sang Soo Soo
Do Joong Dan
Mahk Kee*
Step forwards
with the right
foot and
execute a
double knife
hand middle
block in back
stance.

⓲ *Soo Do Joong
Dan Mahk Kee*
Step backwards
with the right
foot into back
stance, cross the
right hand over
the left arm and
execute a left
knife hand
middle block.

⓳ *Soo Do Sang
Dan Mahk Kee*
Shift the right
foot to the back
of the left foot
and use both
hands to
execute a high
block with the
palms facing
away from the
body (right in
front of left).

20 *Yup Podo Cha Kee [Ki-ahp]* Execute a side snap kick with the right foot, simultaneously pulling both hands down to the left side, and **shout.**

21 *Sang Soo Soo Do Joong Dan Mahk Kee* Look to the left and turn 180° to the left to face south with the left foot forwards. Execute a double knife hand middle block in back stance.

22 *Sang Soo Soo Do Joong Dan Mahk Kee* Step forwards with the right foot and execute a double knife hand middle block in back stance.

23 Preparation movement Pull the right foot back so that both feet are together, clench both fists and lower them down to the front of the body.

24 Preparation movement Raise both arms above the head, fists clenched, with the palms facing south.

25 *Yang Pal Sang Dan Mahk Kee* Pull the fists apart to execute a double block.

123

㉖ *Yang Soo Kwon Do Kong Kyuk*
Circle the arms around, step forwards with the right foot into a front stance, and execute a double outside to inside attack.

㉗ *Joong Dan Kong Kyuk*
Jump forwards, land with the right foot forwards, and execute a jabbing middle punch with the right fist in front stance.

㉘ *Ha Dan Kwan Soo Kong Kyuk*
Look to the left and turn 180° to the left to face north. Shift the left foot forwards into front stance and execute a low right hand knife attack, with the palm at 45° and the left fist striking over the right shoulder.

㉙ *Sang Dan/Ha Dan Mahk Kee*
Pull the left foot back into back stance and execute a high inside to outside block with the right arm and a low block with the left arm.

㉚ *Sang Dan/Ha Dan Mahk Kee*
Shift the left foot next to the right foot with both legs straight. Apply hip twist whilst maintaining the position of both arms.

㉛ *Bal Ba Dahk Euro Mahk Kee*
Execute an outside to inside blocking kick with the right foot to the north.

32 Preparation movement Balance on the left leg with the left knee slightly bent. The arms are crossed (right arm over the left) ready to execute the next movement.

33 *Ha Dan Mahk Kee* Step down with the right foot into horse stance and execute a low block with the right arm.

34 Preparation movement Maintaining the same stance, turn 180° to face south and extend the left open hand at shoulder height towards the south.

35 *Bal Ba Dahk Euro Mahk Kee* Execute an outside to inside blocking kick with the right foot to strike the left open hand and hold the position.

36 *Pal Koop Kong Kyuk* Step down with the right foot into horse stance and execute a right elbow attack to strike the left open palm.

37 *Ha Dan/Joong Dan Mahk Kee* Maintaining the same stance, execute a low block with the right arm and a middle block with the left arm.

38 *Ha Dan/Joong Dan Mahk Kee* Maintaining the same stance, execute a low block with the left arm and a middle block with the right arm.

39 *Ha Dan/Joong Dan Mahk Kee* Maintaining the same stance, again execute a low block with the right arm and a middle block with the left arm.

40 Preparation movement Pivot on both feet and change into a right leg front stance to face south. Bring both fists to the left side and maintain the same height.

41 *Sang Dan/Joong Dan Kong Kyuk* From the same position, execute a high punch with the left fist and a middle punch with the right fist in front stance.

42 Preparation movement Pull the right foot back to the side of the left foot and bring both fists to the right side while applying hip twist.

43 *Bal Ba Dahk Euro Mahk Kee* Execute an outside to inside blocking kick with the left foot and hold the position for the next move.

44 *Sang Dan/Ha Dan Kong Kyuk*
Step forwards with the left foot into front stance and execute a high punch with the right fist and a middle punch with the left fist.

45 Preparation movement
Pull the left foot back to the side of the right foot and bring both fists to the left side while applying hip twist.

46 *Bal Ba Dahk Euro Mahk Kee*
Execute an outside to inside blocking kick with the right foot and hold the position.

47 *Sang Dan/Ha Dan Kong Kyuk*
Step forwards with the right foot in front stance and execute a high punch with the left fist and a middle punch with the right fist.

48 *Ha Dan Mahk Kee*
Look to the left and turn 270° to the left, with the body facing west and eyes focusing north, in a long front stance with the right toes digging into the ground. Execute a low back fist attack with the right hand.

㊾ *Ha Dan Mahk Kee*
Turn 180° to the right, still looking to the north with the body facing east, in a long front stance with the left toes digging into the ground. Execute a low back fist with the left hand.

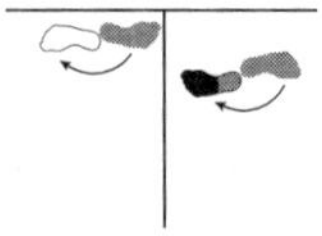

㊿ *Sang Soo Soo Do Joong Dan Mahk Kee*
Half step towards the right foot with the left foot, then shift the right foot forwards into back stance and execute a double knife hand middle block to the north.

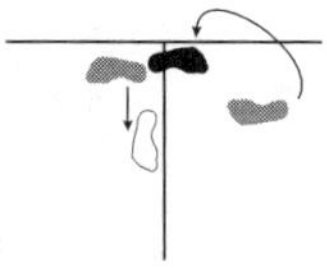

(51) *Sang Soo Soo Do Joong Dan Mahk Kee*
Look to the east, turn 90° to the right into back stance and execute a double knife hand middle block.

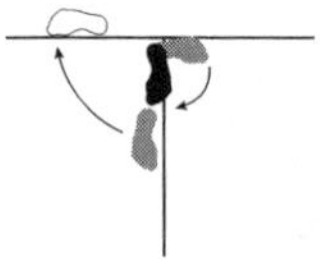

(52) *Sang Soo Soo Do Joong Dan Mahk Kee [Ki-ahp]*
Look to the north, step forwards to the north with the right foot and then step forwards with the left foot into back stance, execute a double knife hand middle block and **shout.**

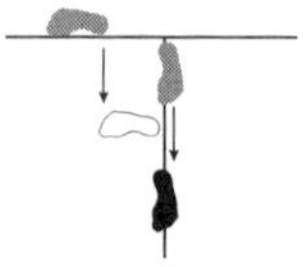

Ba Sa Hee Ba-ro Jase
Pull the left foot back so that both feet are together, with the right fist clenched by the left hand, in return stance.

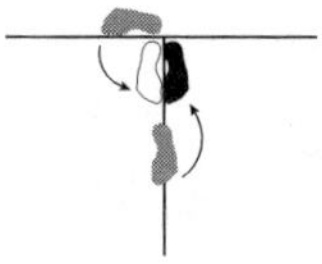

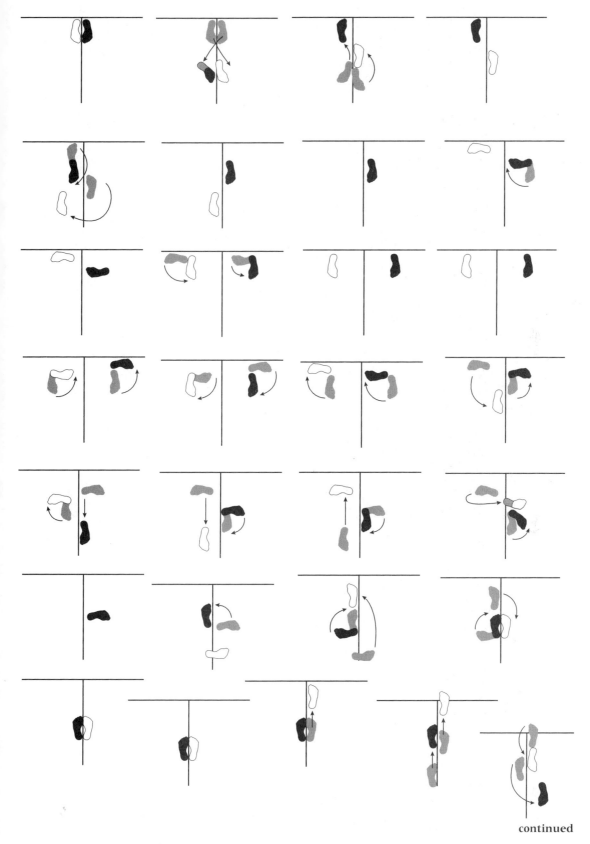

continued

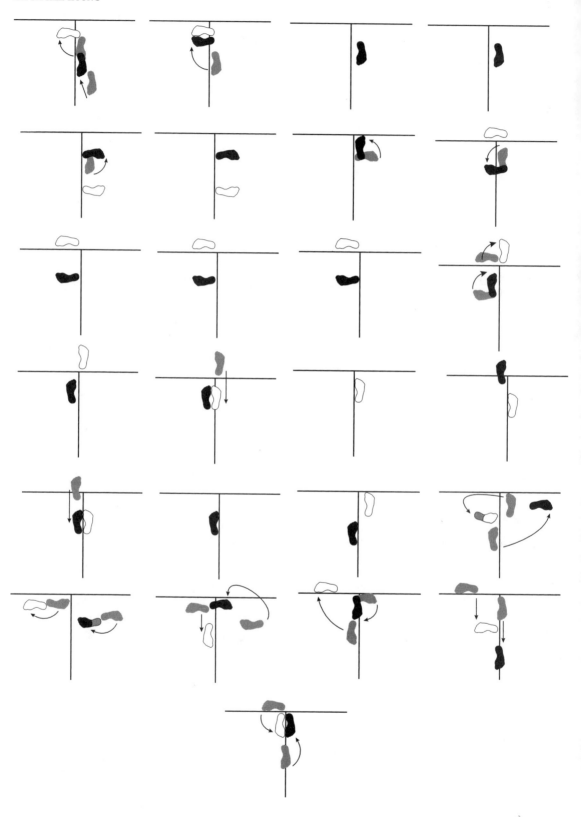

Chil Sung Hyung

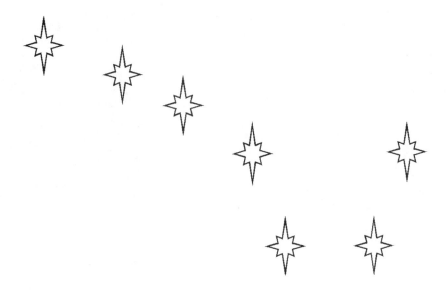

The Chil Sung (seven stars of the Plough) Hyung was devised by Grand Master Hwang Kee in the latter half of the 1980s. It is so-called because Grand Master Hwang Kee's mother was said to have dreamt about the seven stars of the Plough prior to conceiving Hwang Kee. It contains a large number of moves, many of which are found only within this Hyung. Chil Sung Hyung symbolises the Stars.

Chil Sung Il Ro Hyung

Chil Sung I (35 movements)

Chil Sung Il Ro Hyung Direction

RIGHT 1st LINE — BACK — LEFT 1st LINE

RIGHT

CENTRE LINE

LEFT

RIGHT 2nd LINE — FRONT — LEFT 2nd LINE

Joon Bee Jase
Ready stance.

❶ Preparation movement
Look to the left and turn 90° to the left to face west, left foot forwards, in side stance. The left hand should be opened and stretched to the front over the left thigh, with the right hand opened and stretched to the side. Inhale.

❷ *Han Pal Ahn Euro Ahn Ko, Han Pal Son Bah Dak Euro Noo Roo Kee*
Slowly exhale and at the same time move the left hand to the front of the body and move the right hand to the right hip, while slowly changing into front stance.

❸ *Soo Do Kong Kyuk*
Slowly inhale and at the same time cross both arms in front of the body (left arm over the right), and slowly exhale while moving the left knife hand sideways and the right forearm in front of the solar plexus, turning into side stance.

❹ *Joong Dan Kong Kyuk*
Step forwards with the right foot and execute a middle punch with the right hand in front stance.

❺ *Ha Dan Yuk Soo Do Mahk Kee* Look to the right and turn 180° to the east, right foot forwards, in back stance but with the right heel on the ground, the right knee locked and the toes pointing upwards. Execute a low ridge hand block with the right hand with the left forearm protecting the solar plexus.

❻ *Soo Do Kong Kyuk* Slowly inhale and at the same time cross both arms in front of the body (right arm over the left), then slowly exhale while moving the right knife hand sideways and the left open hand in front of the solar plexus, and turning into side stance.

❼ *Joong Dan Kong Kyuk* Step forwards with the left foot and execute a middle punch with the left fist in front stance.

❽ Preparation movement Look to the left and turn 90° to face the north, left foot forwards, in side stance. The left hand should be opened and stretched to the front over the left thigh, with the right hand opened and stretched to the side. Inhale.

❾ *Han Pal Ahn Euro Ahn Ko, Han Pal Son Bah Dak Euro Noo Roo Kee* Slowly exhale and at the same time move the left hand to the front of the body and move the right hand to the right hip, slowly changing into front stance.

❿ *Joong Dan Yuk Mahk Kee* Step forwards with the right foot and execute an inside to outside middle block with the right arm in back stance.

⓫ *Sang Soo Joong Dan Soo Do Mahk Kee*
Step forwards with the left foot and execute a double knife hand middle block in back stance.

⓬ *Hoeng Jin Kong Kyuk [Ki-ahp]*
Step forwards with the right foot into side stance, side punch with the right fist and **shout.**

⓭ *Ho Hoop Dong Jak*
Look to the left and turn 270° from the left to face the east, left foot forwards and both hands in front with the right hand holding the left, in front stance. Scoop inwards with both hands, inhale, lock the left knee and bend the right knee. Exhale, pushing clenched hands forwards, and slowly change into front stance.

⓮ *Yang Pal Kyo Cha Soo Do Mahk Kee*
Maintaining the same stance, cross both arms with elbows nearly touching at chest height, and slowly bring both hands around so that the open palms face towards you.

⓯ *Sang Dan/Ha Dan Mahk Kee*
Drop the right hand down and the left hand to the right shoulder. Quickly execute a 90° knife hand block to the rear of the head with the right hand, and a left arm low knife hand block to the front, moving into back stance.

⓰ *Joong Dan Kong Kyuk*
Step forwards with the right foot and execute a middle punch with the right fist in front stance.

134

❶⑦ *Ho Hoop Dong Jak*
Look to the right and turn 180° to face the west, right foot forwards, both hands in front with the left hand holding the right, in front stance. Scoop inwards with both hands, inhale, lock the right knee and bend the left knee. Exhale, pushing clenched hands forwards, and change into front stance.

⑱ *Yang Pal Kyo Cha Soo Do Mahk Kee*
Maintaining the same stance, cross both arms with elbows nearly touching in front of the body, then slowly bring both hands around so that the open palms face towards you.

⑲ *Sang Dan/Ha Dan Mahk Kee*
Drop the left hand down and the right hand to the left shoulder, then quickly execute a 90° knife hand block to the rear of the head with the left hand, and a right arm low knife hand block to the front, moving into back stance.

⑳ *Joong Dan Kong Kyuk*
Step forwards with the left foot and execute a middle punch with the left fist in front stance.

㉑ *Ha Dan Mahk Kee*
Look to the left and turn 90° to face the south, left foot forwards. Execute a low block with the left arm in front stance.

㉒ *Han Son Joong Dan Soo Do Mahk Kee*
Maintaining the same stance, immediately execute a knife hand middle block with the left hand in front stance (movements ㉑ and ㉒ are to be executed in quick succession).

23 *Joong Dan Kong Kyuk* Step forwards with the right foot and execute a middle punch with the right fist in front stance.

24 *Sang Dan Mahk Kee* Immediately execute a high block with the right arm while remaining in front stance.

25 *Joong Dan Kong Kyuk* Step forwards with the left foot and execute a middle punch with the left fist in front stance.

26 *Sang Dan Mahk Kee* Immediately execute a high block with the left arm in front stance.

27 *Joong Dan Kong Kyuk [Ki-ahp]* Step forwards with the right foot, execute a middle punch with the right fist in front stance and shout.

28 *Sang Soo Ha Dan Noo Roo Kee* Push both hands downwards (palms facing down), straighten the right knee and bend the left knee.

㉙ Pushing movement
Shift into side stance and inhale slowly while pulling both open palms up to chest height. Slowly exhale and push both hands forwards, changing into front stance.

㉚ *Sang Soo Joong Dan Mahk Kee*
Look to the left and turn 270° to face west, left foot forwards. Execute a double arm middle block in front stance.

㉛ *Sang Soo Ha Dan Noo Roo Kee*
Push both hands downwards (palms facing down), straighten the left knee and bend the right knee.

㉜ Pushing movement
Shift into side stance and inhale slowly while pulling both open palms up to chest height. Slowly exhale and push both hands forwards, changing into front stance.

㉝ *Sang Soo Joong Dan Mahk Kee*
Look to the right and turn 180° to face the east, right foot forwards. Execute a double arm middle block in front stance.

㉞ *Sang Soo Ha Dan Noo Roo Kee*
Push both hands downwards (palms facing down), straighten the right knee and bend the left knee.

35 Pushing movement
Shift into side stance and inhale slowly while pulling both open palms up to chest height. Slowly exhale and push both hands forwards, changing into front stance.

Ba-ro Jase
Look to the left and turn 90° to face the north, pulling the right leg back into ready stance.

138

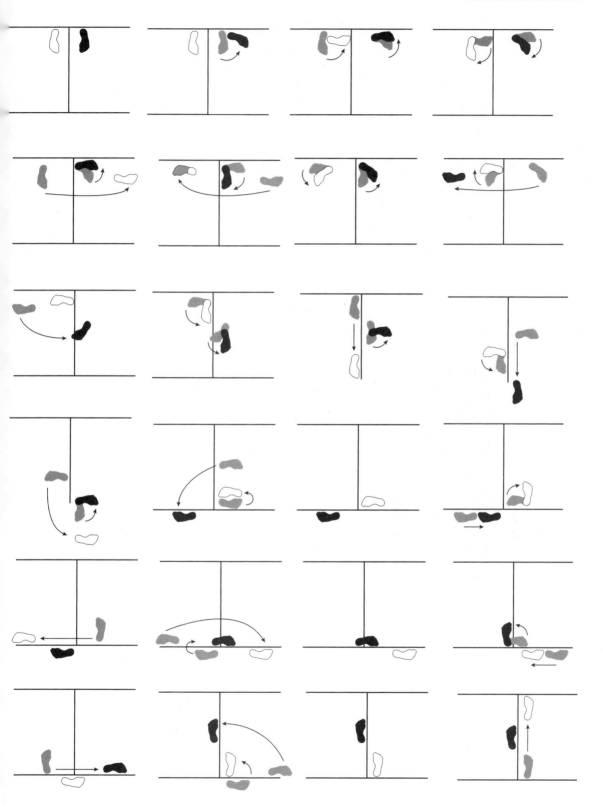

continued

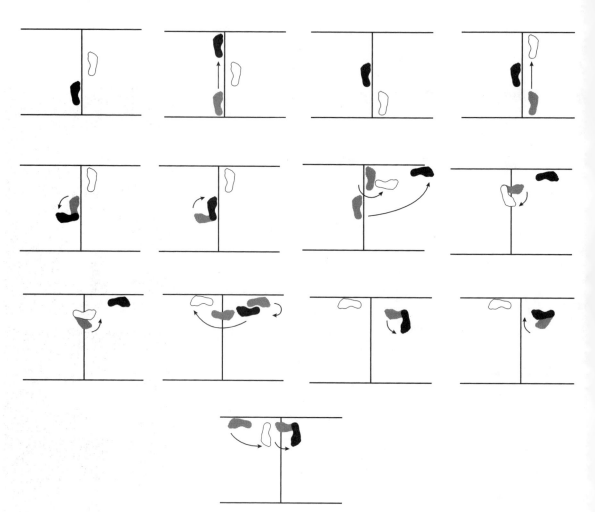

Chil Sung Ee Ro Hyung

Chil Sung II (31 movements)

Chil Sung Ee Ro Hyung Direction

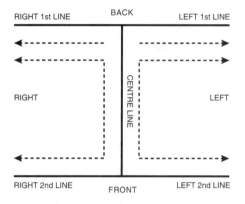

RIGHT 1st LINE — BACK — LEFT 1st LINE

CENTRE LINE

RIGHT — LEFT

RIGHT 2nd LINE — FRONT — LEFT 2nd LINE

Joon Bee Jase
Ready stance.

❶ *Ha Dan Mahk Kee*
Look to the left and turn 90° to face the west. Step forwards with the left leg into front stance and execute a left arm low block.

❷ *Tro Sang Dan Soo Do Kong Kyuk*
Maintaining the same stance, execute a reverse high knife hand attack with the right arm while pulling the left fist to the left side.

❸ *Moo Roop Chee Kee*
Raise both open hands upwards as if to hold an opponents head and immediately execute a right knee attack while pulling down with both hands. Then balance on the left leg while still focusing to the west.

❹ *Kwan Soo Kong Kyuk*
While balancing on the left leg, strike out with a left spear hand attack.

141

❺ *Joong Dan Kong Kyuk*
Step forwards with the right foot into right leg front stance. At the same time, execute a right arm middle punch.

❻ *Tro Joong Dang Kong Kyuk*
Maintaining the same stance, immediately execute a reverse middle punch with the left arm.

❼ *Ha Dan Mahk Kee*
Look over the right shoulder and turn 180° to face the east in right leg front stance. Execute a right arm low block.

❽ *Tro Sang Dan Soo Do Kong Kyuk*
Maintaining the same stance, execute a reverse high knife hand attack with the left arm while pulling the right fist to the right side.

❾ *Moo Roop Cha Kee*
Raise both open hands upwards as if to hold an opponent's head and immediately execute a left knee attack while pulling down with both hands. Then balance on the right leg, still focusing east.

❿ *Kwan Soo Kong Kyuk*
While balancing on the right leg, strike out with a right spear hand attack.

⑪ *Joong Dan Kong Kyuk*
Step forwards with the left foot into left leg front stance. At the same time, execute a left arm middle punch.

⑫ *Tro Joong Dan Kong Kyuk*
Maintaining the same stance, immediately execute a reverse middle punch with the right arm.

⑬ *Sang Soo Joong Dan Mahk Kee*
Look 90° to the left to face north, shift the left leg into left leg front stance and execute a double arm middle block.

⑭ *Hoeng Jin Kong Kyuk*
Looking to the north, shift the right leg forwards into side stance and execute a right arm side punch.

⑮ *Hoeng Jin Kong Kyuk*
Still looking to the north, shift the left leg forwards into side stance and execute a left arm side punch.

⑯ *Hoeng Jin Kong Kyuk [Ki-ahp]*
Still looking to the north, shift the right leg forwards into side stance, execute a right arm side punch and **shout.**

17 *Sang Soo Joong Dan Soo Do Mahk Kee*
Look to the left and turn 270° to the left to face the east in right leg back stance. Immediately execute a double knife hand middle block.

18 *Joong Dan Kong Kyuk*
Step forwards with the right leg into front stance and execute a right arm middle punch.

19 *Sang Soo Joong Dan Soo Do Mahk Kee*
Look to the right and turn 180° to the right to face the west in left leg back stance. Immediately execute a double knife hand middle block.

20 *Joong Dan Kong Kyuk*
Step forwards with the left leg into front stance and execute a left arm middle punch.

21 Preparation movement
Look to the left to face the south and turn 90° to the left into left leg front stance. Simultaneously cross both open hands in front of the face and bring them apart at eye level.

22 *Joong Dan Ap Podo Cha Kee*
Execute a middle front snap kick with the right foot and simultaneously clench both fists, pulling them to the ribcage with the palms facing the body.

㉓ Preparation movement
Step forwards into right leg front stance, cross both open hands in front of the face and bring them apart at eye level.

㉔ *Joong Dan Ap Podo Cha Kee*
Execute a middle front snap kick with the left foot and simultaneously clench both fists, pulling them to the ribcage with the palms facing the body.

㉕ Preparation movement
Step forwards into left leg front stance, cross both open hands in front of the face and bring them apart at eye level.

㉖ *Joong Dan Ap Podo Cha Kee*
Execute a middle front snap kick with the right foot and simultaneously clench the right fist, pulling it back to the right side of the body. The left hand should remain in the same position. After performing the kick, pull the right foot back and balance on the left leg.

㉗ *Joong Dan Kong Kyuk [Ki-ahp]*
Step forwards with the right leg into front stance, immediately execute a right arm middle punch and **shout.**

145

28 *Ha Dan Mahk Kee*
Look to the left and turn 270° to the left to face the west, left leg forwards, in back stance. Immediately execute a left arm low block.

29 *Sang Dan Kong Kyuk*
Step forwards into right leg front stance and execute a right hand high punch.

30 *Ha Dan Mahk Kee*
Look to the right and turn 180° to the right to face the east in left leg back stance. Immediately execute a right arm low block.

31 *Sang Dan Kong Kyuk*
Step forwards into left leg front stance and execute a left hand high punch.

Ba-ro Jase
Look to the left to face the north and pull the left leg back into ready stance.

146

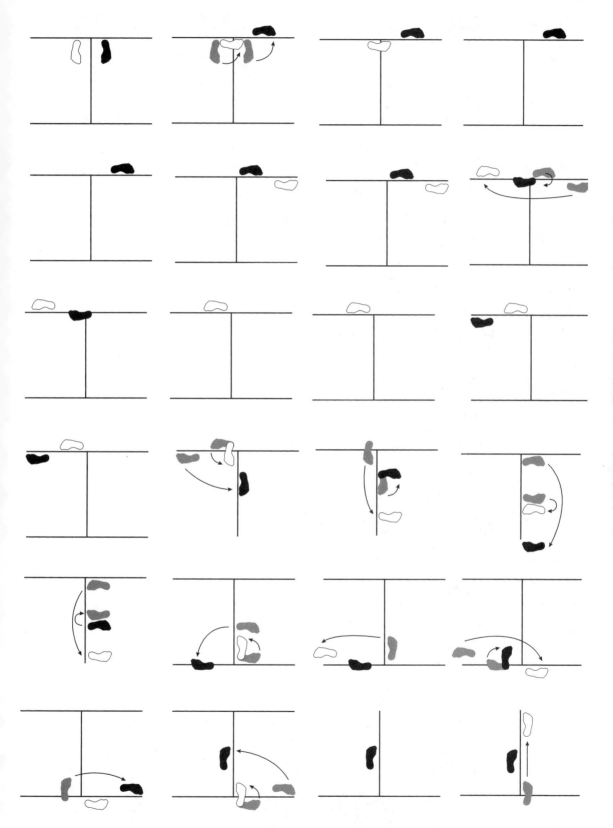

continued

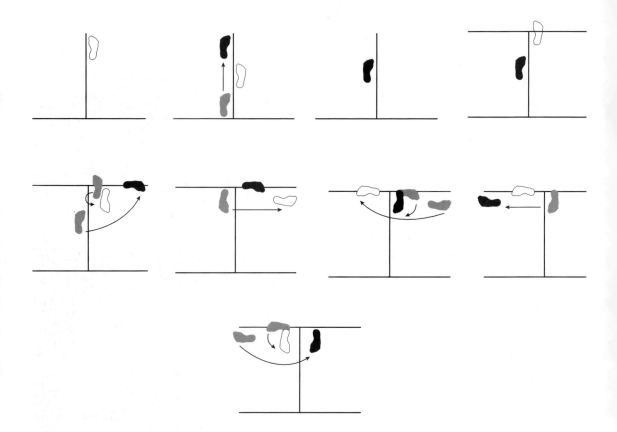

Chil Sung Sam Ro Hyung

Chil Sung III (49 movements)

Chil Sung Sam Ro Hyung Direction

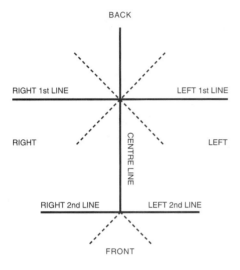

BACK

RIGHT 1st LINE — LEFT 1st LINE

RIGHT — CENTRE LINE — LEFT

RIGHT 2nd LINE — LEFT 2nd LINE

FRONT

Joon Bee Jase
Ready stance.

❶ *Bal Ja Ba Mahk Kee*
Pull both open hands to either side of the waist, inhale, then step forwards with the left foot and bring the right foot behind the left foot with both knees bent. Simultaneously execute a double hand low block with both palms downwards, facing north, and exhale.

❷ Preparation movement
Raise both arms in front of the body until they are above the head, palms facing each other, and at the same time slowly inhale and straighten the knees. Twist both hands to face away from each other then slowly bring both open hands in a circular movement to either side of the body to prepare for the next movement.

❸ Pushing movement Step forwards with the right foot into side stance, slowly push both open palms forwards and exhale. Simultaneously change stance into right leg front stance.

❹ *Soo Do Sang Dan/ Ha Dan Mahk Kee* Step backwards with the right foot into right leg back stance and execute a right arm 90° knife hand block to the rear of the head, simultaneously executing a left arm knife hand low block to the front.

❺ *Joong Dan Ahn Ye Seo Bahk Euro Mahk Kee* Look to the left to face west and shift the left leg into left leg front stance. Execute a left arm inside to outside middle block.

❻ *Tro Joong Dan Ahn Ye Seo Bahk Euro Mahk Kee* Quickly following the previous movement, execute a reverse right arm inside to outside middle block, still looking west in front stance.

❼ *Yup Podo Cha Kee* Execute a right leg side snap kick bringing both open hands to the left hip.

❽ *Soo Do Sang Dan/Ha Dan Mahk Kee* Step back with the right leg into right leg back stance and execute a right arm knife hand high block. At the same time execute a left arm knife hand middle block with both palms facing north.

❾ *Joong Dan Ahn Ye Seo Bahk Euro Mahk Kee*
Look to the right to face east and shift the right leg into right leg front stance. Execute a right arm inside to outside middle block.

❿ *Tro Joong Dan Ahn Ye Seo Bahk Euro Mahk Kee*
Quickly following the previous movement execute a reverse left arm inside to outside middle block, still looking east in front stance.

⓫ *Yup Podo Cha Kee*
Execute a left leg side snap kick bringing both open hands to the right hip.

⓬ *Soo Do Sang Dan/ Ha Dan Mahk Kee*
Step back with the left leg into left leg back stance and execute a left arm knife hand high block. At the same time execute a right arm knife hand middle block with both palms facing north.

⓭ Preparation movement
Look to the left, shift the right foot and turn 135° to face north-west in a side stance. Simultaneously cross both open hands and then bring them apart so that both palms are facing away from the body.

⓮ *Tro Joong Dan Kong Kyuk/Sang Dan Mahk Kee*
Step forwards with the right leg into front stance. Simultaneously execute a left arm reverse middle upper cut attack with the palm facing upwards, and a right arm high block.

151

⓯ *Soo Do Sang Dan/ Ha Dan Mahk Kee*
Jump backwards (still focusing north-west) and land on the right leg, bringing the left foot behind the right knee and balance. At the same time, execute a right arm 90° knife hand block to the rear of the head and a left arm knife hand low block to the front.

⓰ Preparation movement
Step forwards with the left leg into side stance and bring both open hands to the right side. Then slowly change stance into front stance and push both hands forwards with the palms facing north-west, away from the body.

⓱ Preparation movement
Look to the right, bring the left foot together with the right foot and then step out with the right foot into side stance, facing north-east. Simultaneously cross both open hands and then bring them apart so that both palms are facing away from the body.

⓲ *Tro Joong Dan Kong Kyuk/Sang Dan Mahk Kee*
Step forwards with the left leg into front stance. Simultaneously execute a right arm reverse middle upper cut attack with the palm facing upwards, and a left arm high block.

⓳ *Soo Do Sang Dan/ Ha Dan Mahk Kee*
Jump backwards (still focusing north-east) and land on the left leg, bringing the right foot behind the left knee and balance. At the same time, execute a left arm 90° knife hand block to the rear of the head and a right arm knife hand low block to the front.

㉓ Preparation movement
Step forwards with the right leg into side stance and bring both open hands to the left side. Then slowly change stance into front stance and push both hands forwards with palms facing north-east, away from the body.

㉑ *Sang Soo Joong Dan Soo Do Mahk Kee*
Look to the left, shift the right leg and turn 135° to face west in left leg back stance. Execute a double arm knife hand middle block.

㉒ *Sang Soo Joong Dan Soo Do Mahk Kee*
Look to the left and turn 45° to face south-west, stepping forwards with the left leg into back stance. Execute a double arm knife hand middle block.

㉓ *Sang Soo Joong Dan Soo Do Mahk Kee*
Look to the left, shift the left leg and turn 135° to face east in right leg back stance. Execute a double arm knife hand middle block.

㉔ *Sang Soo Joong Dan Soo Do Mahk Kee*
Look to the right and turn 45° to face south-east, stepping forwards with the right leg into back stance. Execute a double arm knife hand middle block.

㉕ *Han Son Joong Dan Soo Do Mahk Kee*
Look to the right and turn 45° to face south, stepping forwards with the right leg into front stance. Execute a right arm knife hand middle block.

㉖ *Sang Soo Ha Dan Mahk Kee*
Step forwards with the left leg into front stance, bring both fists to the right side of the waist and execute a low section cross X block.

㉗ *Sang Soo Sang Dan Mahk Kee*
Step forwards with the right leg into front stance and raise both arms upwards in front of the body to execute a double high block.

㉘ *Yang Soo Kwon Do Kong Kyuk*
Step forwards with the left leg into front stance, circle both arms down and execute a double arm hammer fist attack.

㉙ *Joong Dan Kong Kyuk*
Step forwards with the right leg into front stance and execute a right arm middle punch.

㉚ *Tro Joong Dan Kong Kyuk [Ki-ahp]*
Maintaining the same stance, execute a left arm reverse middle punch and **shout.**

㉛ *Sang Dan/Ha Dan Soo Do Mahk Kee*
Maintaining front stance, look to the left and focus to the north, twisting only the body. Simultaneously execute a right arm knife hand high block and a left arm knife hand low block to the north.

㉜ *Tro Soo Do Sang Dan Kong Kyuk/Sang Dan Mahk Kee*
Shift the left foot slightly and turn the body to face north in a left leg front stance. Simultaneously execute a right arm knife hand high attack and a left arm knife hand high block.

33 *Sang Dan Ap Podo Cha Kee*
Execute a right leg high front snap kick, then balance on the left leg with the right knee held at chest height and both arms in the same position as the previous movement.

34 *Kap Kwon Kong Kyuk [Ki-ahp]*
Jump forwards, land on the right leg and bring the left foot behind the right foot with both knees bent. Execute a right arm back fist attack and **shout.**

35 *Sang Soo Joong Dan Soo Do Mahk Kee*
Jump backwards with the left leg into left leg back stance and execute a double knife hand middle block.

36 *Jang Kwan Mahk Kee*
Step forwards with the left leg into side stance and execute a palm attack with the left arm, focusing north.

37 *Jang Kwan Mahk Kee*
Step forwards with the right leg into side stance and execute a palm attack with the right arm, focusing north.

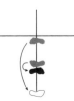

38 *Kwan Soo Kong Kyuk*
Step forwards with the left leg into front stance and execute a spear hand attack with the left arm, keeping the right knife hand on the right side of the waist, palm facing the body.

155

39 *Tro Kwan Soo Kong Kyuk*
Maintaining front stance, execute a reverse spear hand attack with the right arm, keeping the left knife hand on the left side of the waist, palm facing the body.

40 *Ha Dan Yuk Soo Do/ Soo Do Kong Kyuk*
Look to the right, and turn 90° to face east, pivoting on both feet into front stance. Simultaneously execute a left arm knife hand low attack to the front and a right arm knife hand low attack to the rear.

41 *Ha Dan Yuk Soo Do/Soo Do Kong Kyuk*
Maintaining the same stance, quickly execute a right arm knife hand low attack to the front and a left arm knife hand low attack to the rear.

42 *Ha Dan Yuk Soo Do/Soo Do Kong Kyuk*
Look to the left, turn 180° to face west and shift the left foot into front stance. Simultaneously execute a left arm knife hand low attack to the front and a right arm knife hand low attack to the rear.

43 *Ha Dan Yuk Soo Do/Soo Do Kong Kyuk*
Maintaining the same stance, quickly execute a right arm knife hand low attack to the front and a left arm knife hand low attack to the rear.

44 *Sang Dan Mahk Kee*
Look north-west and pull the left foot together with the right foot before stepping out with the left leg into front stance, still facing north-west. Simultaneously execute a left arm high block.

45 *Joong Dan/Ha Dan Mahk Kee/Kong Kyuk* Maintaining the same stance, execute a right arm middle block/attack and a left arm low block/attack, focusing north-west.

46 *Joong Dan/Ha Dan Mahk Kee/Kong Kyuk* Maintaining the same stance, execute a left arm middle block/attack and a right arm low block/attack, focusing north-west.

47 *Sang Dan Mahk Kee* Look to the right and turn 90° to face north-east. Bring the left foot together with the right foot and then step forwards with the right leg into front stance to face north-east. Execute a right arm high block.

48 *Joong Dan/Ha Dan Mahk Kee/Kong Kyuk* Maintaining the same stance, execute a left arm middle block/attack and a right arm low block/attack, focusing north-east.

49 *Joon Dan/Ha Dan Mahk Kee/Kong Kyuk[Ki-ahp]* Maintaining front stance, execute a right arm middle block/attack and a left arm low block/attack, focusing north-east, and **shout**.

Ba-ro Jase Look to the left to face north and pull the left leg back into ready stance.

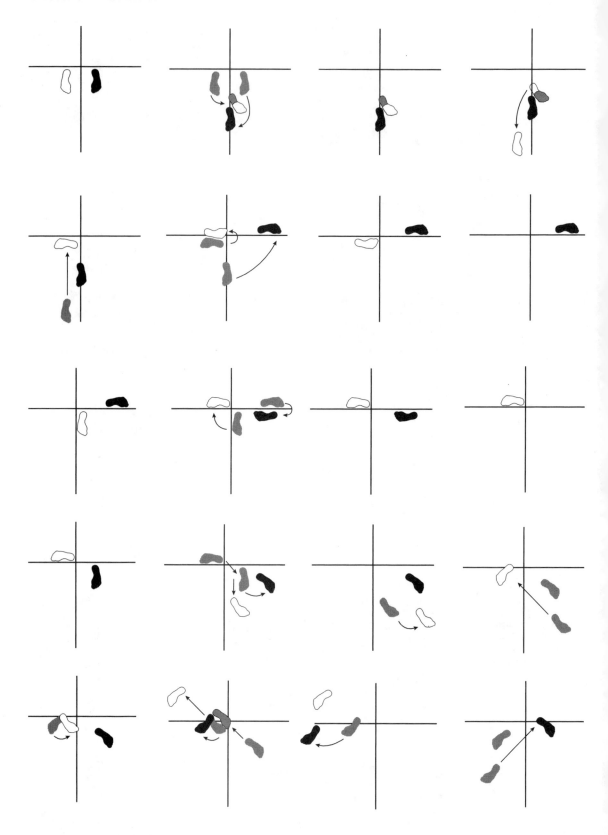

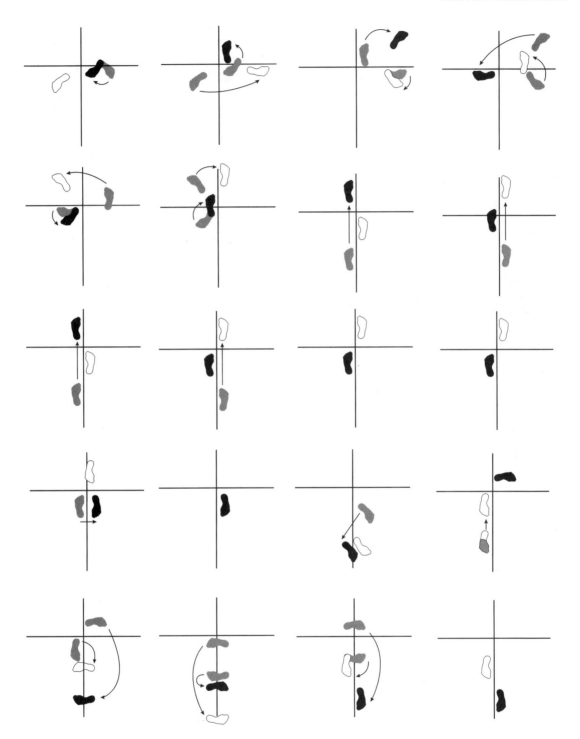

continued

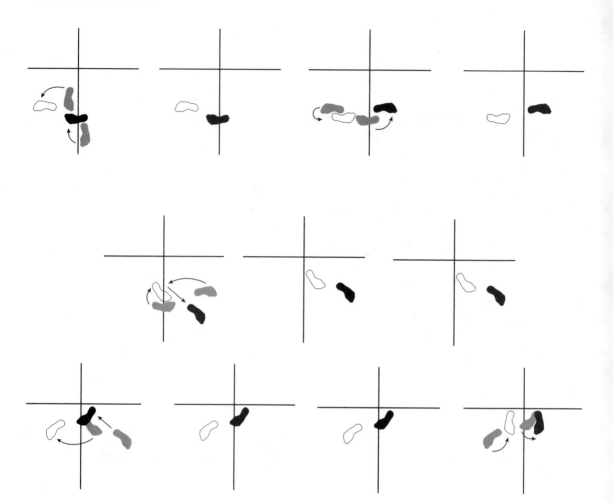

Naihanji Hyung

The Naihanji Hyung was devised 950 years ago, during the era of the Song Dynasty, by the founder of the Kang Woo Ryu school of martial arts. It is characterised by a horse riding posture in all movements, with both feet placed toe-in. Naihanji Hyung symbolises the Horse.

Naihanji Cho Dan Hyung

Naihanji form I (27 movements)

Naihanji Cho Dan Hyung
Direction

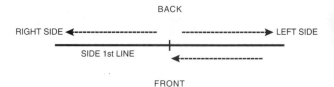

BACK

RIGHT SIDE ◀----------------------   ----------------------▶ LEFT SIDE

SIDE 1st LINE   ◀----------------------

FRONT

*Naihanji Cho
Dan Joon Bee
Jase*
Ready stance.
Place the left
hand on top of
the right hand,
with both feet
together, facing
north.

❶ *Yang Soo Ha
Dan Mahk Kee*
Drop to the
right into a
crossed leg
stance with
both knees bent
(left foot in
front of right
foot), still look-
ing north.

❷ Preparation
movement
Turn 90° to face
east and extend
the right open
hand at
shoulder height,
pulling the left
fist to the left
side. Shift the
right foot into
horse stance.

❸ *Pal Koop Kong Kyuk* Still in horse stance, execute an elbow attack with the left elbow to contact the right open palm.

❹ Preparation movement Focus north, still in horse stance, and bring both fists to the right side.

❺ *Ha Dan Mahk Kee* Turn 90° to face west, still in horse stance, and low block with the left arm.

❻ *Joong Dan Kong Kyuk* Immediately execute a right hand punch (can be used as a middle block) at chest height with the elbow slightly bent, pulling the left fist to the left side.

❼ *Joong Dan Mahk Kee/Kong Kyuk* Step across to the west (right foot in front of left foot) then step out with the left foot to land in horse stance. At the same time, execute a right hand inside to outside middle block/back fist attack while looking north.

❽ *Ha Dan Mahk Kee/Kong Kyuk* Simultaneously execute a left hand low block/punch to the north and a right fist high punch to the left shoulder.

❾ *Ha Dan/Sang Dan Mahk Kee* Execute a low block to the right side with the right arm and a right-angled high block to the left side with the left arm.

❿ *Joong Dan Mahk Kee/Kong Kyuk* Execute an outside to inside block/back fist attack with the left arm, and a right arm middle block (right fist underneath the left elbow, palm facing down). Movements ❽, ❾ and ❿ to be executed in quick succession.

⓫ *Joong Dan Mahk Kee/Kong Kyuk* Focusing 90° west, lift the left foot up to the right knee before stamping back down into horse stance. Execute a middle double arm inside to outside block/back fist attack to the left, maintaining the position of the arm.

⓬ *Joong Dan Mahk Kee/Kong Kyuk* Focusing 180° east, lift the right foot up to the left knee before stamping back down into horse stance. Executing a middle outside to inside double arm block/attack to the right, maintaining the position of the arm.

⓭ Preparation movement Focusing north, move both fists to the right side of the waist with the right palm facing upwards and the left palm facing down, keeping both fists level.

14 *Kwon Do Kong Kyuk [Ki-ahp]*
Focusing 90° west, execute a
hammer punch to the west with
the left fist, middle block with the
right arm in front of the chest (both
palms facing down) and **shout**.

15 Preparation
movement
Still in horse
stance and
focusing west,
extend the left
open hand at
shoulder height
and shift the
right fist to the
right side of the
waist.

16 *Pal Koop
Kong Kyuk*
Execute a right
arm elbow
attack to the left
open palm, still
maintaining
horse stance
and focusing
90° west.

17 Preparation
movement
Focus north,
still in horse
stance, and
bring both fists
to the left side.

18 *Ha Dan
Mahk Kee*
Focus 90° east,
still in horse
stance, and low
block with the
right arm.

19 *Joong Dan Kong Kyuk*
Immediately execute a left hand punch at chest height with the elbow slightly bent, pulling the right fist to the right side.

20 *Joong Dan Mahk Kee/Kong Kyuk*
Step across to the right (left foot crosses in front of right), then step out with the right foot to land in horse stance. At the same time execute a left hand inside to outside middle block/back fist attack, looking north.

21 *Ha Dan Mahk Kee/Kong Kyuk*
Execute a right hand low block/punch to the north and at the same time a left fist high punch to the right shoulder.

22 *Ha Dan/Sang Dan Mahk Kee*
Execute a low block to the left side with the left arm and a right-angled high block to the right side with the right arm.

23 *Joong Dan Mahk Kee/Kong Kyuk*
Execute an outside to inside block/back fist attack with the right arm and move the left fist underneath the right elbow, palm facing down. (Movements **21**, **22** and **23** to be executed in quick succession.)

24 *Joong Dan Mahk Kee/Kong Kyuk*
Focusing 90° east, lift the right foot up to the left knee before stamping back down into horse stance. Execute a middle inside to outside double arm block/back fist attack to the right, maintaining the position of the arm.

25 *Joong Dan Mahk Kee/Kong Kyuk*
Focusing 180° west, lift the left foot up to the right knee before stamping back down into horse stance. Execute a middle outside to inside double arm block/back fist attack to the left, maintaining the position of the arm.

26 Preparation movement
Focusing north, move both fists to the left side of the waist with the left palm facing upwards and the right palm facing down, keeping both fists level.

27 *Kwon Do Kong Kyuk [Ki-ahp]*
Focusing 90° east, execute a hammer punch to the east with the right fist and a middle block with the left fist in front of the chest (both palms facing down), and **shout.**

Ba-ro Jase
Look north and pull the right foot back into ready stance with the left hand on top of the right hand, feet together, facing north.

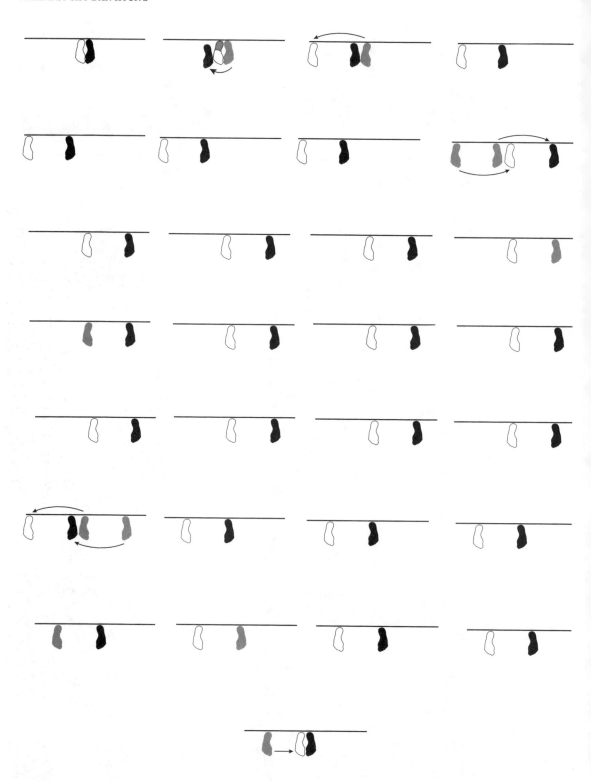

Naihanji Ee Dan Hyung

Naihanji form II (30 movements)

Naihanji Ee Dan Hyung Direction

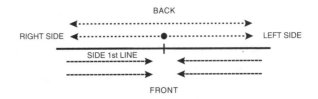

Joon Bee Jase
Ready stance.

❶ *Mok Jo Roo Kee*
Looking north, step to the right with the left foot (left foot in front of right foot) with both knees bent into a crossed leg stance. Both arms are crossed at the wrists at face height before being pulled down and outwards to shoulder height. The arms should be at a 45° angle (movement to grab an opponents collar), with the body weight on the left foot.

❷ *Sang Dan Mahk Kee/Kong Kyuk*
Look east, lift the right leg and stamp the right foot down into horse stance. Execute a right arm side block/attack with the left arm protecting the middle area, the right palm facing east, and the left palm facing downwards.

❸ *Ha Dan Mahk Kee*
Look north and step to the right with the left foot (left foot in front of right foot) with both knees bent into a crossed leg stance. At the same time, pull the right fist from the rear of the body to the groin area (palm facing forwards), with the left open hand covering the right wrist.

169

❹ *Joong Dan Mahk Kee/Kong Kyuk*
Look east, lift the right leg and stamp the right foot down into horse stance. Execute a right arm middle block/back fist attack with left open hand at the left side of the right fist.

❺ *Mok Jo Roo Kee*
Look north and step to the left with the right foot (right foot in front of left foot) with both knees bent into a crossed leg stance. Both arms are crossed at the wrists at face height, before being pulled down and outwards to shoulder height. The arms should be at a 45° angle (movement to grab an opponents collar), with the body weight on the right foot.

❻ *Joong Dan Mahk Kee/Kong Kyuk*
Look west, lift the left leg and stamp the left foot down into horse stance. Execute a left arm middle block/attack with the right arm protecting the middle area, the left palm facing west, and the right palm facing downwards.

❼ *Ha Dan Mahk Kee*
Look north, step to the left with the right foot (right foot in front of left foot) with both knees bent into a crossed leg stance. At the same time, pull the left fist from the rear of the body to block the groin area (palm facing forwards), with the right open hand covering the left wrist and the weight on the right foot.

❽ *Joong Dan Mahk Kee/Kong Kyuk*
Look west, lift the left leg and stamp the left foot down into horse stance. At the same time execute a left arm middle block/back fist attack with right open hand at the right side of the left fist.

❾ Preparation movement
Look north, pull the left fist to the side of the body with the right open hand covering the front of the fist and the right forearm protecting the solar plexus, in horse stance.

❿ *Joong Dan Mahk Kee/Kong Kyuk*
Still in horse stance, look east and execute a right arm middle block/back fist attack with left open hand at the left side of the right fist.

⓫ Preparation movement
Looking north, lift the right leg to the side of the left knee and balance on the left leg. At the same time, bring the right fist to the side of the body with the left open hand supporting the front of the right fist.

⓬ *Sang Soo Pal Koop Kong Kyuk [Ki-ahp]*
Stamp down with the right foot back into horse stance. Simultaneously twist the upper body anti-clockwise and execute elbow attacks with both elbows at shoulder height, with the right hand on the fist and left open palm supporting the right fist and **shout.**

⓭ *Joong Dan Soo Do Mahk Kee*
Still in horse stance, look east, drop the right hand to the left hip and execute a middle right arm knife hand block, bringing the left fist to the side of the body to prepare for the next movement.

⓮ *Joong Dan Kong Kyuk/Mahk Kee*
Looking east, execute a middle punch/block with the left arm, with the elbow slightly bent, the left forearm protecting the solar plexus and the right fist at the right side.

⓯ Preparation movement
Step to the right with the left foot (left foot in front of right foot) into a crossed leg stance, with the weight on the left foot.

16 *Joong Dan Mahk Kee/Kong Kyuk*
Look north, lift the right leg and stamp it back down into horse stance. Simultaneously execute a middle inside to outside block/back fist attack with the left arm, with the right fist at the side of the body.

17 *Ha Dan Mahk Kee/Kong Kyuk*
Execute a low section block/attack to the groin area with the right arm. Simultaneously execute a left fist high punch to the right shoulder to prepare for the next movement (movements **17** to **19** are to be executed with speed).

18 *Joong Dan/Ha Dan Mahk Kee/Kong Kyuk*
Execute a high right-angled block/attack with the right arm and a low block/attack to the left side with the left arm.

19 *Sang Soo Joong Dan Mahk Kee/Kong Kyuk*
Execute a right arm outside to inside block/back fist attack, with the left arm protecting the solar plexus and the left fist positioned underneath the right elbow, palm downwards.

20 Preparation movement
Still looking north and standing in horse stance, pull the right fist to the right side and move the left open palm to support the front of the right fist.

21 *Joong Dan Mahk Kee/Kong Kyuk*
Look west and execute a left arm middle block/back fist attack with the right open hand at the right side of the left fist.

㉒ Preparation movement
Looking north, lift the left leg to the side of the right knee and balance on the right leg. At the same time, bring the left fist to the side of the body with the right open hand supporting the front of the left fist.

㉓ *Sang Soo Pal Koop Kong Kyuk [Ki-ahp]*
Stamp down with the left foot back into horse stance. Twist the upper body clockwise, execute elbow attacks with both elbows at shoulder height, the left hand in a fist with the right open palm supporting the left fist, and **shout**.

㉔ *Joong Dan Soo Do Mahk Kee*
Still in horse stance, look west, drop the left hand to the right hip and execute a middle left arm knife hand block, bringing the right fist to the side of the body to prepare for the next movement.

㉕ *Joong Dan Kong Kyuk/ Mahk Kee*
Execute a middle punch with the right arm with the elbow slightly bent and the forearm of the right arm protecting the solar plexus. Move the left fist to the left side.

㉖ Preparation movement
Step to the left with the right foot (right foot in front of left foot) into a crossed leg stance, keeping the weight on the right foot.

㉗ *Joong Dan Mahk Kee/Kong Kyuk*
Look north, lift the left leg and stamp it back down into horse stance. Execute a middle inside to outside block/back fist attack with the right arm, with the left fist at the side of the body.

173

28 *Ha Dan Mahk Kee/Kong Kyuk*
Still looking north, execute a low section block/attack to the groin area with the left arm. Then execute a right fist high punch to the left shoulder to prepare for the next movement (movements **28** to **30** are to be executed with speed).

29 *Sang Dan Mahk Kee/Kong Kyuk*
Execute a high right-angled block/attack with the left arm and a low block/attack to the right side with the right arm.

30 *Sang Soo Joong Dan Mahk Kee/Kong Kyuk*
Execute a left arm outside to inside block/back fist attack with the right arm protecting the solar plexus and the right fist positioned underneath the left elbow.

Ba-ro Jase
Pull the left foot back into ready stance.

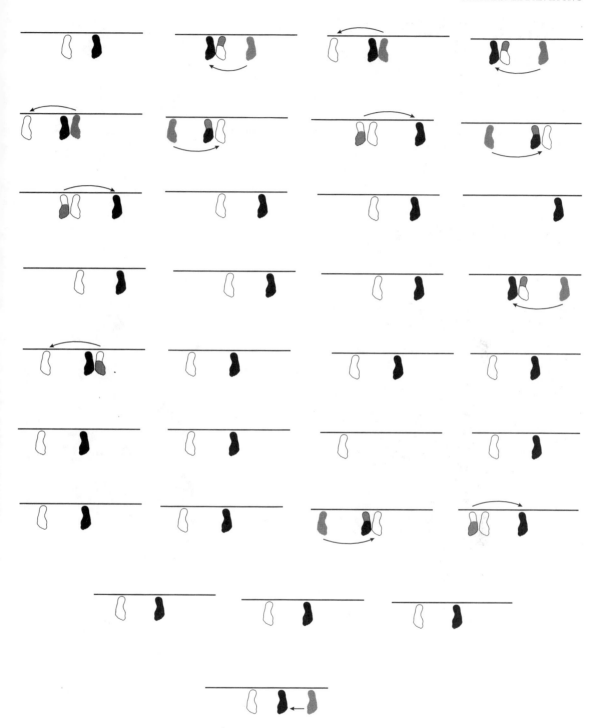

Naihanji Sam Dan Hyung

Naihanji form III (40 movements)

Naihanji Sam Dan Hyung Direction

BACK

RIGHT SIDE   ----------------------► LEFT SIDE

SIDE 1st LINE
◄----------•••••••••••••••••••••••••••••••►

FRONT

Joon Bee Jase
Ready stance.

❶ *Joong Dan/Ha Dan Ahn Ye Seo Bahk Euro Mahk Kee*
Shift the right foot to the right into horse stance and simultaneously execute a middle inside to outside block/back fist attack with the left arm and a low inside to outside block/attack with the right arm, looking north.

❷ *Joong Dan/Ha Dan Ahn Ye Seo Bahk Euro Mahk Kee*
Still in horse stance, simultaneously execute a middle inside to outside block/back fist attack with the right arm and a low inside to outside block/attack with the left arm.

❸ Preparation movement
Pull the right fist to the left shoulder.

❹ *Sang Dan/Ha Dan Mahk Kee/Kong Kyuk* Execute a right-angled block/back fist attack to the right side with the right arm and a low block to the left side with the left arm.

❺ *Joong Dan Bahk Ye Seo Ahn Euro Mahk Kee/Kong Kyuk* Execute an outside to inside middle block/back fist attack with the right fist, keeping the left fist underneath the right elbow, protecting the solar plexus.

❻ *Sang Dan/Ha Dan Mahk Kee/Kong Kyuk* Step to the right with the left foot (left in front of right) into a crossed foot stance. Simultaneously execute a high right-angled block/back fist attack to the right side with the right arm and a low block/attack to the left side with the left arm, keeping the weight on the left foot.

❼ *Bahk Ye Seo Ahn Euro Mahk Kee/Joong Dan Mahk Kee/Kong Kyuk* Execute an outside to inside middle block/back fist attack with the right fist, keeping the left fist underneath the right elbow, protecting the solar plexus. Step to the right into horse stance and look north.

❽ Preparation movement Pull the right fist to the right side (right palm facing upwards) with the left hand open and in front of the right fist.

❾ *Joong Dan Kong Kyuk* Execute a middle punch with the right fist and simultaneously shift the left open hand over the right elbow.

❿ Twist movement Still in horse stance and looking north, keep the left palm still and quickly twist the right fist so that the palm now faces upwards.

⓫ Preparation movement Look east and step to the right side with the left foot (left foot in front of right foot) into a crossed leg stance, keeping the weight on the left foot. Bring the right fist to shoulder height.

⓬ *Ha Dan Mahk Kee/ Kong Kyuk* Step to the right with the right foot into horse stance. Execute a low block/attack to the right side with the right palm facing upwards and the right arm supported by the left open hand, to the left side of the right fist, looking east.

⓭ Circular block/attack Still in horse stance and looking east, execute a complete 360° anti-clockwise circular block/attack to stop at the original position; at the same time, twist the right fist so that the palm now faces downwards with the left hand still at the left side of the right fist.

14 *Joong Dan Soo Do Mahk Kee* Look west and execute an open knife hand middle block with the left arm, pulling the right fist to the right side, in horse stance.

15 *Joong Dan Kong Kyuk* Quickly execute a middle punch with the right arm with the elbow slightly bent and the forearm protecting the solar plexus. Simultaneously pull the left fist back to the left side, in horse stance, looking west.

16 Preparation movement Step to the west with the right foot (right foot in front of left) into a crossed leg stance, and at the same time move the left fist to the right shoulder (palm facing downwards) and the right arm to the left side of the waist, looking west and keeping the weight on the right foot.

17 *Ahn Ye Seo Bahk Euro Joong Dan Mahk Kee* Step with the left foot into horse stance and execute an inside to outside block/back fist attack with the right arm, pulling the left fist to the left side.

18 *Sang Dan/Ha Dan Mahk Kee/Kong Kyuk* Execute a low block/attack with the left arm, and at the same time a high attack over the left shoulder with the right fist.

19 *Sang Dan/Ha Dan Mahk Kee/Kong Kyuk* Still in horse stance and looking north, execute a high right-angled block/back fist attack with the left arm and a low block/attack to the right side with the right arm.

179

20 *Bahk Ye Seo Ahn Euro Joong Dan Mahk Kee* Execute an outside to inside middle block/back fist attack with the left arm, with the right fist underneath the left elbow and the right arm protecting the solar plexus.

21 *Joong Dan/Ha Dan Ahn Ye Seo Bahk Euro Mahk Kee* Simultaneously execute a middle inside to outside back fist attack with the right arm and a low inside to outside block/attack with the left arm, looking north.

22 *Joong Dan/Ha Dan Ahn Ye Seo Bahk Euro Mahk Kee* Still in horse stance, simultaneously execute a middle inside to outside block/back fist attack with the left arm and a low inside to outside block/attack with the right arm.

23 Preparation movement Pull the left fist to the right shoulder.

24 *Sang Dan/Ha Dan Mahk Kee/Kong Kyuk* Execute a right-angled block/back fist attack to the left side with the left arm, and a low block to the right side with the right arm.

㉕ *Joong Dan Bahk Ye Seo Ahn Euro Mahk Kee/Kong Kyuk*
Execute an outside to inside middle block/back fist attack with the left fist, with the right fist underneath the left elbow, protecting the solar plexus.

㉖ *Sang Dan/Ha Dan Mahk Kee/Kong Kyuk*
Still looking north, step to the left with the right foot (right in front of left) into a crossed foot stance. Simultaneously execute a high right-angled block/back fist attack to the left side with the left arm and a low block/ attack to the right side with the right arm, keeping the weight on the right foot.

㉗ *Bahk Ye Seo Ahn Euro Joong Dan Mahk Kee*
Execute an outside to inside middle block/ back fist attack with the left fist, with the right fist under- neath the left elbow, protect- ing the solar plexus. Step to the left into horse stance and look north.

㉘ Preparation movement
Pull the left fist to the left side (left palm facing upwards) with the right open hand in front of the left fist.

㉙ *Joong Dan Kong Kyuk* Execute a middle punch with the left fist and simultaneously shift the right open hand over the left elbow.

㉚ Twist movement Still in horse stance and looking north, keep the right palm still and quickly twist the left fist so that the palm now faces upwards.

㉛ Preparation movement Look west and step to the left side with the right foot (right foot in front of left foot) into a crossed leg stance, keeping the weight on the right foot. Bring the left fist to shoulder height.

㉜ *Ha Dan Mahk Kee/ Kong Kyuk* Step to the left with the left foot into horse stance. Execute a low block/ attack to the left side, with the left palm facing upwards and the left arm supported by the right open hand, to the right side of the left fist, looking west.

㉝ Circular block/attack Still in horse stance and looking west, execute a complete 360° clockwise circular block/attack to stop at the original position; at the same time twist the left fist so that the palm now faces downwards with the right hand still at the right side of the left fist.

34 *Joong Dan Soo Do Mahk Kee*
Look east and execute an open knife hand middle block with the right arm, pulling the left fist to the left side, in horse stance.

35 *Joong Dan Kong Kyuk*
Quickly execute a middle punch with the left arm, with the elbow slightly bent and the forearm protecting the solar plexus. Simultaneously pull the right fist back to the right side, in horse stance, looking east.

36 Preparation movement
Step to the east with the left foot (left foot in front of right foot) into a crossed leg stance. At the same time move the right fist to the left shoulder (palm facing downwards) and the left arm to the right side of the waist, looking east and keeping the weight on the left foot.

37 *Ahn Ye Seo Bahk Euro Joong Dan Mahk Kee*
Step with the right foot into horse stance and execute an inside to outside block/back fist attack with the left arm, pulling the right fist to the right side.

38 *Sang Dan/Ha Dan Mahk Kee/Kong Kyuk*
Execute a low block/attack with the right arm, and at the same time a high attack over the right shoulder with the left fist.

39 *Sang Dan/Ha Dan Mahk Kee/Kong Kyuk*
Still in horse stance and looking north, execute a high right-angled block/back fist attack with the right arm and a low block/attack to the left side with the left arm.

40 *Bahk Ye Seo Ahn Euro Joong Dan Mahk Kee*
Execute an outside to inside middle block/back fist attack with the right arm, with the left fist underneath the right elbow and the left arm protecting the solar plexus, and **shout**.

Ba-ro Jase
Pull the right foot back into ready stance.

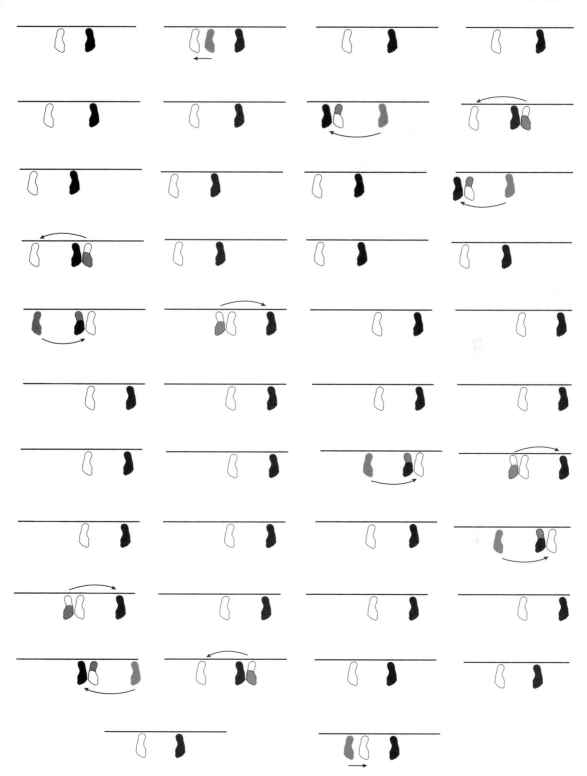

185

Ship Soo (Jin Thwe) Hyung

Also known as Jit Dae, this Hyung originates from the
Ha Book region of China. The originator is unknown. It is
characterised by having only a small number of moves,
practised in a slow dignified manner with concentrated
power. Ship Soo Hyung is particularly suitable for people
with a large physique, or holders of the 4th or 5th Dan,
and symbolises the Bear.

Ship Soo (Jin Thwe) Direction

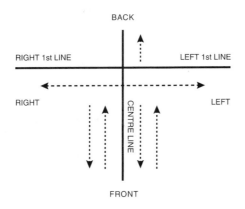

Ship Soo (Jin Thwe) Hyung

(27 movements)

Ship Soo Joon Bee Jase
Shift both feet together and bring both hands up to chin height. Clench the right hand into a fist, with the left hand open and holding the right fist, and the left thumb slightly inserted into the right fist.

❶ Slow blocking motion
Shift the left foot back into front stance. Simultaneously move the right arm (open hand) to the right side with the arm extended to the rear, whilst closing the left fist. Inhale. Then slowly and simultaneously move the right arm forwards and shift the left fist to the left side. Exhale.

❷ Slow blocking motion
Step forwards with the left foot into side stance, with the body facing north-east, move the left open hand to a low position under the right arm and move the right open hand to the left side of the body at shoulder height. Inhale as this is performed. Then slowly move the right hand down to the right side to end with the palm facing downwards and the fingers pointing 45° north-east, and move the left hand up to chin height with the palm facing upwards. Exhale as this is performed. At the same time, change into front stance.

❸ *Han Son Joong Dan Soo Do Mahk Kee*
Slowly execute a left arm middle knife hand block (palm facing down) whilst maintaining the same stance as in the previous movement.

❹ *Soo Do Ahn Ye Seo Bahk Euro Mahk Kee/Kong Kyuk*
Shift the right foot to the east into left leg back stance and execute a right arm inside to outside block/reverse palm attack. At the same time, bring the left fist to the left side.

❺ *Jang Kwan Mahk Kee/Kong Kyuk*
Look to the north, move the right foot into side stance and execute a middle section open hand block/attack to the shoulder with the right arm.

❻ *Jang Kwan Mahk Kee/Kong Kyuk*
Move the left foot forwards into side stance and execute a middle open hand block/attack to the shoulder with the left arm.

❼ *Jang Kwan Mahk Kee/Kong Kyuk*
Move the right foot forwards into side stance and execute a middle open hand block/attack to the shoulder with the right arm.

❽ *Sang Soo Sang Dan Mahk Kee*
Look to the west and shift the right foot to the left (left foot behind the right foot) into a crossed leg stance, simultaneously executing a high double arm crossed block.

❾ *Sang Soo Ha Dan Mahk Kee*
Focus to the south and move the left foot into side stance before looking to the west and executing a double low block with both arms to either side of the body.

❿ *E Dan*
Focus and jump to the south with both feet off the ground. At the same time, cross both arms in front of the body at head height in preparation for the next movement.

⓫ *Yang Soo Sang Dan Mahk Kee/Kap Kwon Kong Kyuk*
After landing, look to the west and execute a double arm 90° block/back fist attack to both sides of the head whilst in side stance.

⓬ *Yang Soo Sang Dan Mahk Kee*
Look to the north and move the left foot forwards into side stance. Leave both arms in the same position as the previous movement whilst applying hip twist and focusing to the east.

⓭ *Yang Soo Sang Dan Mahk Kee*
Look to the north and move the right foot to the north into side stance. Leave both arms in the same position as the previous movement whilst applying hip twist and focusing to the east.

⓮ *Yang Soo Sang Dan Mahk Kee*
Look to the north and move the left foot to the north into side stance. Leave both arms in the same position as the previous movement whilst applying hip twist and focusing to the east.

⓯ *Sang Soo Sang Dan Mahk Kee*
Still looking to the east, execute a high double arm crossed fist block above the head, inhale and then slowly exhale as the knees are straightened and both arms are slowly brought down to their respective sides of the body and straightened.

⓰ *Han Son Joong Dan Soo Do Mahk Kee*
Look to the south and shift the right foot to the south into front stance. Execute a right open hand middle block whilst the left fist moves to the left side of the body.

⓱ *Bong Eul Yang Son Euro Mahk Kee* (two hand block for stick)
Still in front stance and looking to the south, bring both open hands to the left hip and then move them forwards to complete a defensive position. The right open hand twists so that the palm faces upwards at waist height, with the left open hand facing upwards at a slight angle and the left elbow at the left side of the ribcage. (Movements **⓰** and **⓱** should be executed in quick succession.)

⓲ *Soo Do Sang Dan Mahk Kee*
Pivoting on the right foot, lift the left foot up to the back of the (bent) right knee to complete a one-legged stance. At the same time, twist the body so that it faces west and execute a high open hand 90° block to the rear with the right arm whilst the left open hand protects the solar plexus (palm facing down). Execute a hip twist to finish.

⓳ *Bong Eul Yang Son Euro Mahk Kee* (two hand block for stick)
Step to the south with the left foot into front stance, bring both open hands to the right hip and then move them forwards to complete a defensive position. The left hand twists so that the palm faces upwards at waist height with the right open hand facing upwards at a slight angle and the right elbow at the right side of the ribcage. This movement should be executed slowly.

⓴ *Soo Do Sang Dan Mahk Kee*
Pivoting on the left foot, lift the right foot up to the back of the (bent) left knee to complete a one-legged stance. At the same time, twist the body so that it faces east and execute a high open hand 90° block to the rear with the left arm whilst the right open hand protects the solar plexus (palm facing down). Execute a hip twist to finish.

㉑ *Bong Eul Yang Son Euro Mahk Kee*
(two hand block for stick)
Step to the south with the right foot into forward stance, bring both open hands to the left hip and move them forwards to complete a defensive position. The right hand twists so that the palm faces upwards at waist height with the left open hand facing upwards at a slight angle and the left elbow at the left side of the ribcage. This movement should be executed slowly.

㉒ *Sang Dan/Ha Dan Mahk Kee/Kong Kyuk*
Look to the left, turn 270° to focus west and step forwards with the left leg into back stance. Simultaneously execute a high right-angled block/back fist attack to the rear with the right arm and a low block/attack with the left arm to the front.

㉓ *Sang Dan/Ha Dan Mahk Kee/Kong Kyuk*
Look to the right and turn to the right to face east, shifting the right foot into a right leg back stance. Simultaneously execute a high right-angled block/back fist attack to the rear with the left arm and a low block/attack with the right arm to the front (movements **㉒** and **㉓** are to be executed in quick succession).

㉔ *Sang Dan Mahk Kee*
Look to the left and move the left foot to turn to the north into front stance. Execute a high block with the left arm.

㉕ *Sang Dan Mahk Kee*
Step forwards with the right foot to execute a high block.

㉖ *Sang Dan Mahk Kee (Ki-ahp)*
Look to the left and shift the left foot to face south in front stance. At the same time, execute a high block with the left arm and **shout** (movements **㉕** and **㉖** to be executed in quick succession).

㉗ *Sang Dan Mahk Kee*
Step forwards with the right foot into forward stance and execute a high block with the right arm.

Ship Soo Ba-ro Jase
Look to the left and pivot on the right foot to face north. Bring both feet together and bring both hands up to chin height, the right hand in a fist with the left open hand clenching the right fist and the left thumb slightly inserted into the right fist.

193

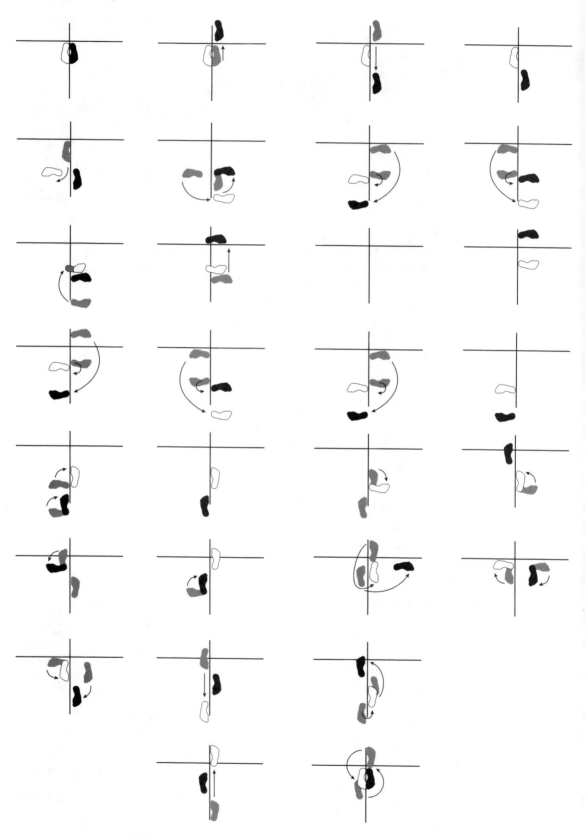

Jin Do Hyung

Jin Do Hyung was originally known as Jin Dwe and was developed in the Ha Nam region of China about 300 years ago. The originator is unknown. It belongs to the So Lim school of martial arts, and consists of many technically demanding and rapid movements.
Jin Do Hyung symbolises the Crane.

Jin Do Hyung Direction

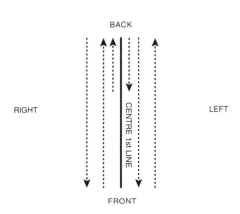

Jin Do Hyung

Jin Do Hyung (44 movements)

Joon Bee Jase
Ready stance.

❶ *Sang Soo Soo Do Sang Dan Mahk Kee*
Step backwards with the right leg into side stance, left foot in front, and move both fists to the right hip before executing a double knife hand cross block above the head, focusing to the north.

❷ Preparation movement
Maintaining the same side stance, pull both hands straight down to the right side of the waist. The right fist is clenched (palm upwards) with the left hand open palm in front of the right fist.

❸ *Soo Do Kong Kyuk*
Still remaining in the same stance, execute a left arm knife hand attack.

❹ *Tro Joong Dan Kong Kyuk*
From the side stance, shift both feet into left leg front stance and simultaneously execute a reverse middle punch with the right arm.

❺ *Bahk Ye Seo Ahn Euro Cha Kee*
Look to the left, lift the right leg and bring it forwards to execute an outside to inside block kick to the south. At the same time, bring the right fist to the left shoulder and the left fist blocking downwards to the front of the body and balance on the left leg.

❻ *Ha Dan Mahk Kee*
Step down with the right leg into side stance (body facing east) and immediately execute a right arm low block, whilst focusing south.

❼ *Sang Soo Soo Do Sang Dan Mahk Kee*
Look to the left to focus north, shift both feet into left leg front stance facing north, and bring both fists to the right hip. Execute a double knife hand X block above the head, focusing straight to the front.

❽ Preparation movement
Maintaining the same front stance, pull both hands down to chest height in the same X block position but clenching the fists.

❾ *Ee Dan Ap Podo Cha Kee*
Lift the right knee, bring it forwards and execute a left leg jumping front snap kick.

❿ *Sang Soo Kyo Cha Ha Dan Mahk Kee*
Land with the left leg forwards in front stance and bring the fists to the right hip. Immediately execute a low double arm X block, focusing straight ahead.

⓫ *Sang Soo Kyo Cha Ha Dan Mahk Kee*
Look to the right, lift the left leg and turn 180° to the right to face south in a left leg front stance, bringing both fists to the right hip. Immediately apply hip twist whilst executing a low double arm X block, focusing south.

197

12 *Yang Soo Ha Dan Mahk Kee*
Look to the right and turn 180° to the right to face north in left leg back stance. Execute a double arm low block with both fists clenched.

13 *Ha Dan Soo Do Mahk Kee*
Step forwards with the left leg into back stance and execute a double arm knife hand low block, focusing north.

14 Preparation movement
Step forwards with the right leg into side stance, facing west. At the same time, bring both open hands up to chest level in an X block position (palms facing the body). Slowly twist the hips into front stance, facing north, simultaneously opening the hands so that the palms

15 *Yang Pal Kyo Cha Soo Do Mahk Kee*
Shift both feet and body into side stance, facing west, and cross both open hands (palms facing upwards) before bringing them apart with the forearms at approximately 45°, focusing west.

16 Preparation movement
Maintaining side stance with both knees bent, bring both fists above the head into a cross block position, before slowly straightening the knees and bringing both fists down to either side of the body, focusing west.

⑰ *Sang Dan/Ha Dan Mahk Kee*
Look left to face south, pull the left foot back into right leg back stance, and execute a 90° block to the rear of the head with the right arm and a low block to the front of the body with the left arm, with clenched fists.

⑱ *Sang Dan/Ha Dan Mahk Kee*
Still facing south, quickly step forwards into left leg back stance and execute a 90° block to the rear of the head with the left arm, and a right arm low block to the front of the body.

⑲ *Sang Dan/Ha Dan Mahk Kee*
Look to the left, turn 180° backwards into right leg back stance and execute a 90° block to the rear of the head with the right arm, and a left arm low block to the front of the body.

⑳ *Sang Soo Ha Dan Mahk Kee*
Quickly focus to the west, step back with the right leg into a west facing front stance and bring both fists to the right hip. Kneel down on the right knee and execute a cross block with both fists, focusing west (movements **⑱**, **⑲** and **⑳** are to be executed in quick succession).

㉑ *Yang Pal Kyo Cha Mahk Kee*
Shift the right leg into side stance, facing west. Cross both fists, palms facing upwards, before bringing them apart with the forearms at approximately 90°, focusing west.

㉒ Preparation movement
Maintaining the same stance with both knees bent, bring both fists above the head to a cross block position, before slowly straightening the knees and bringing both fists down to either side of the body, focusing west.

㉓ *Yang Pal Pal Koop Kong Kyuk*
Maintaining the same stance, bring both fists to the waist on each side of the body and twist the upper body to the left to execute a right elbow block to the front of the body and a left elbow block to the rear.

㉔ *Yang Pal Pal Koop Kong Kyuk*
Quickly twist the upper body to the right and execute a left elbow block to the front of the body and a right elbow block to the rear.

㉕ *Yang Pal Kyo Cha Mahk Kee*
Look to the right, pivot the body on the right foot and bring the left foot behind the right, with both knees bent, focusing east. Simultaneously cross both fists at chest height and then bring them apart, palms facing upwards and the forearms at an angle of about 90°, still focusing east.(Movements **㉓**, **㉔** and **㉕** are to be executed in quick succession.)

㉖ *Sang Soo Sang Dan/ Ha Dan Mahk Kee*
Look to the left to face north, lift the left foot and hold it behind the right knee. Simultaneously execute a 90° block to the rear of the head with the right arm and a low block to the front of the body with the left arm, and balance.

㉗ Preparation movement
Still balancing on the right leg, bring both fists to the right side of the body at waist height and hip twist to prepare for the next move, knees facing forwards.

㉘ *Joong Dan Ap Podo Cha Kee*
From the balanced position, execute a left leg middle front snap kick, simultaneously extending the left hand parallel to the left leg.

㉙ *Joong Dan Kong Kyuk*
Step down with the left leg, then step forwards with the right leg into right leg front stance and simultaneously execute a right arm middle punch, still facing north.

㉚ *Sang Soo Sang Dan/ Ha Dan Mahk Kee*
Lift the right foot, pull it back to the rear of the left knee and balance. Simultaneously execute a 90° block to the rear of the head with the left arm, and a right arm low block to the front of the body.

㉛ Preparation movement
Still balancing on the left leg, bring both fists to the left side of the body at waist height and hip twist to prepare for the next move, knees facing forwards.

㉜ *Joong Dan Ap Podo Cha Kee*
From the balanced position, execute a right leg middle front snap kick, simultaneously extending the right hand parallel to the right leg.

㉝ *Tro Joong Dan Kong Kyuk*
Step down with the right leg into right leg front stance and execute a reverse left arm middle punch.

㉞ *Sang Soo Sang Dan/Ha Dan Mahk Kee*
Look left, turn 180° to face south, lift the left foot and hold it behind the rear of the right knee. Simultaneously execute a 90° block with the right arm and a left arm low block to the front of the body.

35 Preparation movement
Still balancing on the right leg, bring both fists to the right side of the body at waist height and hip twist to prepare for the next move, knees facing forwards.

36 *Joong Dan Ap Podo Cha Kee*
From the balanced position, execute a left leg middle front snap kick, simultaneously extending the left hand parallel to the left leg.

37 *Tro Joong Dan Kong Kyuk*
Step down with the left leg into left leg front stance and execute a reverse right arm middle punch.

38 *Han Son Soo Do Joong Dan Mahk Kee/Kong Kyuk*
Look to the right and turn 180° to face north. Simultaneously shift the stance into side stance and execute a middle knife hand block/reverse palm attack, whilst bringing the left fist to the left side.

39 *Pal Koop Kong Kyuk*
Maintaining the same stance, move the right open palm to the front of the body and execute a middle section elbow attack with the left

40 Preparation movement
Maintaining the same stance, bring both hands to the left side of the waist, with the left fist clenched and the right hand open in front.

41 *Sang Soo Soo Do Sang Dan Mahk Kee*
Pivot to the right on the right foot, turn to face south, lift the left foot and hold it behind the right knee. Simultaneously execute a double knife hand cross block above the head and balance.

42 Preparation movement
Still balancing on the right leg, bring both hands to the right side of the body at waist height. The left hand should be open, palm facing down, in front of the right clenched fist. Hip twist to prepare for the next move.

43 *Joong Dan Ap Podo Cha Kee*
From the balanced position, execute a left leg middle front snap kick, simultaneously extending the left open hand parallel to the left leg.

44 *Hoeng Jin Kong Kyuk [Ki-ahp]*
Step down with the left leg and slide forwards with the right leg into an east facing horse stance. Execute a side punch with the right arm, looking to the south, and **shout.**

Ba-ro Jase
Return with the left leg to ready stance.

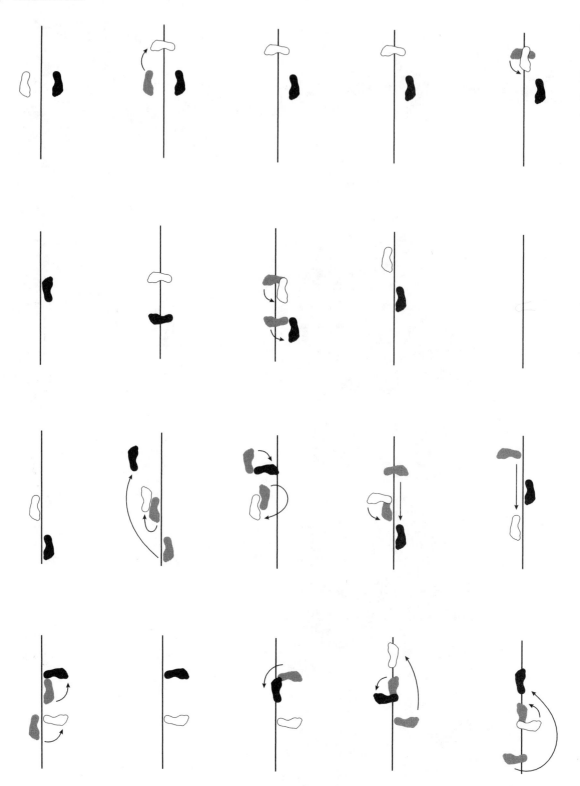

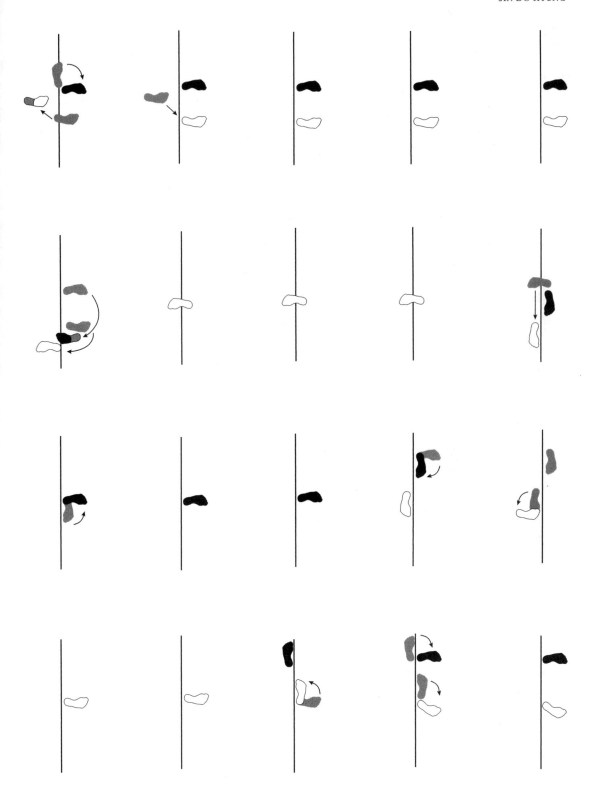

continued

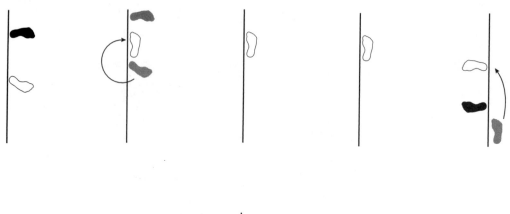

Kong San Goon Hyung

This Hyung was devised by Ggung and Ssang Gween who lived in the Ha Nam region of China, and contains many fascinating, varied and effective movements. The movements portray the repelling of enemies attacking from four directions. It is regarded by many as the Hyung of all Hyungs and symbolises the Eagle.

Kong San Goon (Ggung Ssang Gween) Hyung

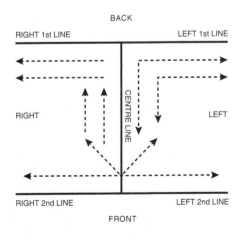

Kong San Goon Hyung

(66 movements)

Joon Bee Jase
Open both hands so that both thumbs and forefingers touch to form a triangle shape.

❶ Preparation movement
Slowly raise both hands above the head. Pause for a moment and then pull both hands apart, slowly circling both arms down each side of the body to about waist height before bringing both open hands together to make contact (right knife hand striking the left palm).

❷ *Sang Dan Soo Do Mahk Kee* Immediately look to the left and step to face the west in a right leg back stance, simultaneously executing a high left arm knife hand block.

❸ *Sang Dan Soo Do Mahk Kee* Quickly following the previous movement, look to the right to face east, shift the stance into left leg back stance and execute a high right arm knife hand block.

❹ Preparation movement Turn 90° to face north and shift both feet into side stance with both hands on the right side at the same level, the right hand in a fist and the left hand open in front of the right.

❺ *Soo Do Kong Kyuk* Immediately execute a middle section knife hand attack with the left arm (the following five movements are to be executed in quick succession).

❻ *Joong Dan Kong Kyuk* Remaining in side stance, quickly execute a middle punch with the right arm.

❼ *Joong Dan Ahn Ye Seo Bahk Euro Mahk Kee* Execute a right arm middle inside to outside block. Simultaneously shift the right foot into front stance, facing north west.

8 *Joong Dan Kong Kyuk* Quickly execute a left arm middle punch and shift stance back into side stance.

9 *Joong Dan Ahn Ye Seo Bahk Euro Mahk Kee* Quickly following the previous movement, execute a left arm middle inside to outside block. Simultaneously shift the left foot into front stance, facing north east.

10 *Sang Soo Joong Dan Soo Do Mahk Kee* Half step with the left foot and then step towards the north with the right leg into left leg back stance. Execute a double knife hand middle block.

11 *Sang Soo Joong Dan Soo Do Mahk Kee* Step forwards with the left leg into right leg back stance and execute a double knife hand middle block.

12 *Kwan Soo Kong Kyuk* Step forwards with the right leg into front stance. Block with the left arm in front of the solar plexus, palm facing downwards, and execute a spear hand attack with the right arm.

13 *Tro Soo Do Sang Dan Kong Kyuk/Sang Dan Mahk Kee* Look to the left and turn 180° to face south. Immediately execute an open hand high block with the left arm and a high right arm knife hand attack in front stance.

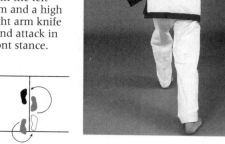

14 *Ap Podo Cha Kee*
Execute a right front snap kick whilst maintaining the same arm positions and focusing south.

15 *Kwan Soo Kong Kyuk*
Step down with the right leg and turn 180° to the left to face north in right leg back stance. Simultaneously execute a low knife hand attack with the right arm, pulling the left fist to the right shoulder.

16 *Sang Dan/Ha Dan Mahk Kee*
Remaining in back stance, execute a 90° block to the rear of the head with the right arm and a left arm low block to the front of the body, with both fists clenched.

17 *Kwan Soo Kong Kyuk*
Remaining in back stance, execute a low knife hand attack with the right arm, pulling the left fist to the right shoulder.

18 Preparation movement
Pull the left foot back together with the right foot with both knees straight. Slowly extend the left arm out to face north whilst pulling the right fist to the right side.

19 *Tro Soo Soo Sang Dan Kong Kyuk/Sang Dan Mahk Kee*
Step forwards with the left leg into front stance and execute a knife hand high block with the left arm, and a high knife hand attack in front stance.

20 *Ap Podo Cha Kee*
Execute a right leg front snap kick whilst maintaining the same arm positions and focusing north.

21 *Kwan Soo Kong Kyuk*
Step down with the right leg and turn 180° to the left to face south in left leg front stance. Simultaneously execute a low knife hand attack with the right arm, pulling the left fist to the right shoulder.

22 *Sang Dan/Ha Dan Mahk Kee*
Pull the left foot backwards into right leg back stance and execute a 90° block to the rear of the head with the right arm, and a left arm low block to the front of the body.

23 *Kwan Soo Kong Kyuk*
Step forwards with the left foot again into front stance and execute a low knife hand attack with the right arm, pulling the left fist to the right shoulder.

24 Preparation movement
Pull the left foot back together with the right foot with both knees straight. Slowly extend the left arm out to face south whilst pulling the right fist to the right side.

25 Preparation movement
Look to the left and turn 90° to face east, lift the left foot and hold it beside the right knee. At the same time, bring both fists to the right side of the body, apply hip twist and balance on the right leg.

㉖ *Yup Podo Cha Kee*
Execute a side snap kick to the east with the left leg and simultaneously execute a left hammer fist, the left arm parallel with the left leg.

㉗ *Pal Koop Kong Kyuk*
Step down with the left leg into front stance to face east and execute an elbow attack with the right elbow, striking the left open palm.

㉘ Preparation movement
Look to the right, turn 180° to face west, lift the right foot and hold it beside the left knee. At the same time, bring both fists to the left side of the body, apply hip twist and balance on the left leg.

㉙ *Yup Podo Cha Kee*
Execute a side snap kick to the west with the right leg and simultaneously execute a right hammer fist, the right arm parallel with the right leg.

30 *Pal Koop Kong Kyuk*
Step down with the right leg into front stance to face west and execute an elbow attack, with the left elbow striking the right open palm.

31 *Sang Soo Joong Dan Soo Do Mahk Kee*
Look to the left and turn 180° to face east into right leg back stance. Simultaneously execute a double knife hand middle block.

32 *Sang Soo Joong Dan Soo Do Mahk Kee*
Turn 45° to the right to face south-east and step with the right leg into left leg back stance. Execute a double knife hand middle block.

33 *Sang Soo Joong Dan Soo Do Mahk Kee*
Look to the right, turn to face west and shift the right leg into back stance. Execute a double knife hand middle block.

34 *Sang Soo Joong Dan Soo Do Mahk Kee*
Turn 45° to the left to face south-west and step with the left leg into right leg back stance. Execute a double knife hand middle block.

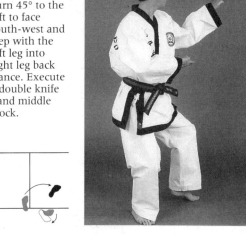

35 *Tro Soo Do Sang Dan Kong Kyuk/Sang Dan Mahk Kee*
Look to the left to face south and step forwards with the left leg into front stance. Simultaneously execute a left arm knife hand high block and a right arm knife hand high attack.

36 *Ap Podo Cha Kee* Execute a right leg front snap kick whilst maintaining the same arm positions and focusing south.

37 *Kap Kwon Kong Kyuk* Hop forwards, land on both feet with the right foot in front of the left, and execute a high back fist attack with the right fist.

38 *Joong Dan Ahn Ye Seo Bahk Euro Mahk Kee* Jump backwards with both legs and shift the stance into right leg front stance. Simultaneously execute a right arm inside to outside middle block.

39 *Tro Joong Dan Kong Kyuk* Maintaining the same stance, execute a reverse middle punch with the left arm.

40 *Joong Dan Kong Kyuk* Remaining in front stance, quickly execute a middle punch with the right arm.

41 Preparation movement Look to the left to face north and turn 180°. Pivot on the left foot, lift the right foot up to the rear of the left knee and balance. Rotate both hands around before making contact in front of the solar plexus at a 90° angle, with the bottom of the right fist striking the left open palm.

42 Jump
Jump as far forwards as possible and land with the right foot forwards in a long front stance. On landing, place both open hands on either side of the body with only the fingertips touching the ground, focusing north.

43 *Chwe Soo Do Ha Dan Mahk Kee*
Look to the left to face south in a very low right leg back stance and execute a low left arm knife hand block, with the right open hand protecting the solar plexus.

44 *Sang Soo Joong Dan Soo Do Mahk Kee*
Step forwards with the right leg into back stance and execute a double knife hand middle block.

45 *Joong Dan Ahn Ye Seo Bahk Euro Mahk Kee*
Look to the left, turn 270° to face west into left leg front stance and execute a left arm inside to outside middle block.

46 *Tro Joong Dan Kong Kyuk*
Maintaining front stance, execute a reverse middle punch with the right arm.

47 *Joong Dan Ahn Ye Seo Bahk Euro Mahk Kee*
Look to the right and turn 180° to face east, pivot into right leg front stance and execute a right arm inside to outside middle block.

48 *Tro Joong Dan Kong Kyuk*
Remaining in front stance, execute a reverse middle punch with the left arm.

49 *Joong Dan Kong Kyuk*
Quickly execute a right arm middle punch whilst maintaining front stance.

50 Preparation movement
Look to the right to face south, lift the right foot up, hold it beside the left knee and balance. Simultaneously pull both fists to the left side and apply hip twist, focusing south.

51 *Yup Podo Cha Kee*
Execute a right leg side snap kick and a right hammer fist, the right arm parallel to the right leg.

52 *Sang Soo Joong Dan Soo Do Mahk Kee*
Step down with the right leg and look left to face north in a right leg back stance. Immediately execute a double middle knife hand block.

53 *Joong Dan Kwan Soo Kong Kyuk*
Step forwards with the right leg in front stance. Block with the left arm in front of the solar plexus, palm facing downwards, and execute a middle spear hand attack with the right arm.

54 Preparation movement
Pull the right hand back and rotate it around the front of the face until the palm is facing away from the face. At the same time, bring the left foot forwards and behind the right foot, with the back turned to the front, whilst focusing north.

55 *Kwon Do Kong Kyuk*
Look to the left, and shift the left leg around to the front into side stance. Execute a left arm hammer attack with the palm of the left hand facing downwards, whilst focusing north.

56 *Kap Kwon Kong Kyuk [Ki-ahp]*
Jump forwards as far as possible, land in side stance, execute a left arm back fist attack and shout, still focusing north.

57 *Pal Koop Kong Kyuk*
Maintaining the same stance, twist the upper body and execute an elbow attack with the right elbow striking the left open palm.

58 Preparation movement
Maintaining the same stance, focus east and bring both fists to the left side of the waist to prepare for the next movement (movements **58** and **59** are to be executed with speed).

59 *Ha Dan Mahk Kee* Maintaining the same stance, look to the south and execute a low block to the right side of the body.

60 *Sang Dan/Ha Dan Mahk Kee* Look to the right and turn the body 180° to face west, stepping with the left leg into side stance. Simultaneously execute a 90° block to the right side of the head with the right arm and a left arm low block to the front of the body.

61 *Sang Soo Kyo Cha* Remaining in the same stance, bring the right hand on top of the left wrist and execute a low X block whilst applying hip twist and focusing west.

62 *Sang Soo Soo Do Sang Dan Mahk Kee* Still in the same position, execute a double cross knife hand high block. Immediately bring both hands down to the chest, the arms still crossed and the fists clenched.

63 *Sang Soo Soo Do Sang Dan Mahk Kee*
Look to the right, shift the left leg and turn 270° into right leg front stance. Execute a double cross knife hand high block.

64 Preparation movement
Remaining in front stance, bring the X block down to the chest and clench both fists.

65 *Ee Dan Ap Podo Cha Kee*
Execute a jumping front snap kick with the right leg whilst facing south.

66 *Joong Dan Ahn Ye Seo Bahk Euro Mahk Kee [Ki-ahp]*
Land with the right leg forwards in front stance, execute an inside to outside middle block with the right arm and **shout**.

Ba-ro Jase
Look to the right and slowly execute a right hand low block on the side of the right leg, then pivot on the right foot to face north in ready stance.

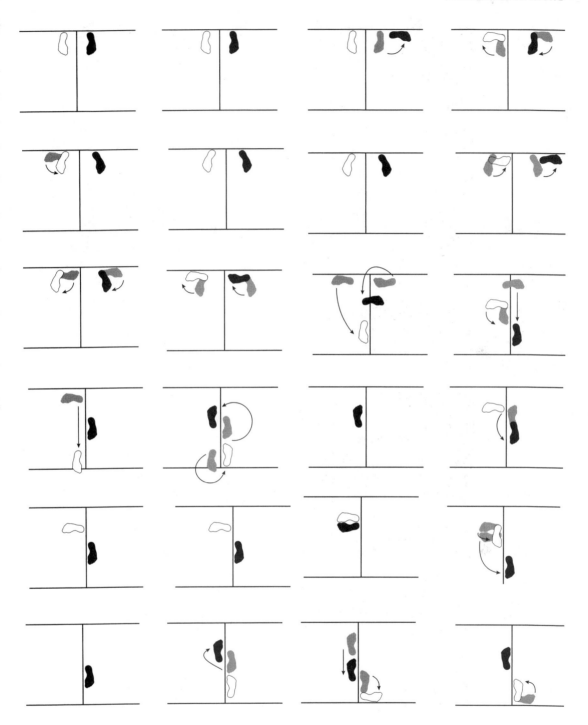

continued

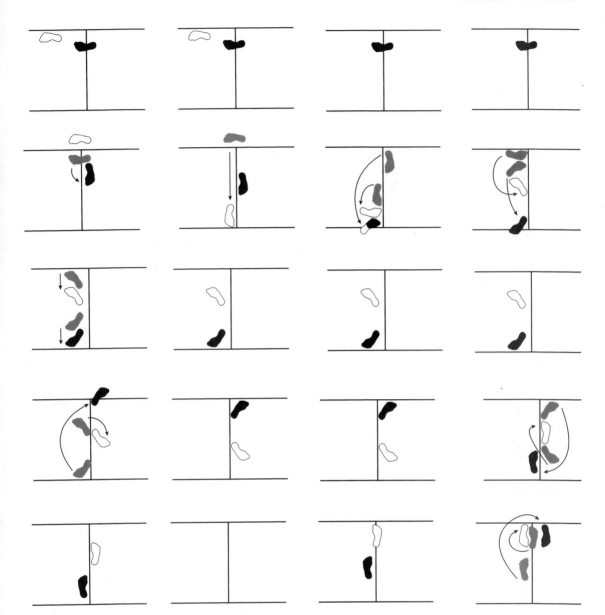

Ro Hai Hyung

Ro Hai Hyung belongs to the So Lim school of martial arts. Its originator is unknown.

Ro Hai Hyung Direction

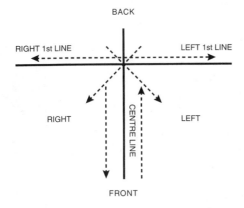

Ro Hai Hyung

(33 movements)

Ro Hai Joon Bee Jase
Open both hands so that both thumbs and forefingers touch to form a triangle shape. Look north.

❶ *Ha Dan Soo Do Mahk Kee*
Look to the right and shift the right foot to the east into left leg back stance. Simultaneously execute a double knife hand low block.

❷ *Ha Dan Yuk Soo Do Mahk Kee*
Look to the left and shift the left foot to the west into right leg back stance. Simultaneously execute a double ridge hand low block with both palms facing upwards.

❸ Preparation movement
Look to the right and shift the left foot so that both feet are together and facing 45° north-east. Simultaneously bring both fists to their respective sides of the body with the palms facing upwards and the knees straightened.

❹ *Eema Kong Kyuk*
Jump forwards in a north easterly direction, land on the right foot with the left foot tucked behind the right knee. Simultaneously execute a forehead attack, bringing both fists to either side of the head with the palms facing towards the head.

❺ *Soo Do Sang Dan/ Ha Dan Mahk Kee*
Jump backwards to land on the left leg (left knee bent) and balance, with the right foot tucked behind the left knee. At the same time, execute a left knife hand right-angled block to the back of the head and a right knife hand low block to the front of the body.

❻ *Han Son Joong Dan Soo Do Mahk Kee*
Step forwards (north-east) with the right leg into front stance and execute a right knife hand middle block, bringing the left fist to the left side.

❼ *Joong Dan Kong Kyuk*
Step forwards (north-east) with the left leg and execute a left arm middle punch in front stance.

❽ *Tro Joong Dan Kong Kyuk*
Still facing north-east and maintaining the same stance, execute a right arm middle punch.

❾ *Ha Dan Mahk Kee*
Look to the left and turn to face the west in left leg front stance. Simultaneously execute a left arm low block.

❿ *Tro Joong Dan Kong Kyuk*
Still facing west, pull the left foot back and change into the right leg back stance. At the same time, execute a reverse middle punch with the right arm with the right elbow slightly bent.

⓫ *Soo Do Sang Dan/ Ha Dan Mahk Kee*
Look to the right, jump backwards and land on the left leg with the right foot tucked behind the left knee. Facing north-west, execute a high right-angled knife hand block to the back of the head with the left arm and a low knife hand block to the front with the right arm.

12 *Han Son Joong Dan Mahk Kee*
Step forwards (north-west) with the right foot into front stance and execute a right arm knife hand middle block while bringing the left fist to the left side.

13 *Joong Dan Kong Kyuk*
Step forwards (north-west) with the left foot into front stance and execute a left arm middle punch.

14 *Tro Joong Dan Kong Kyuk*
Still facing north-west and maintaining the same stance, execute a reverse middle punch with the right arm.

15 Foot strike
Pull the right leg forwards and up to strike the left open hand at knee height with the sole of the right foot. Bring the right fist to the right side to prepare for the next movement whilst looking downwards.

16 Downward punch *[Ki-ahp]*
Shift the right foot back, bending the right knee. Execute a downward punch whilst looking downwards and **shout**.

17 *Soo Do Sang Dan/ Ha Dan Mahk Kee*
Focus forwards and jump backwards onto the left leg with the right foot tucked behind the knee. At the same time, execute a high right-angled knife hand block to the back of the head with the left arm, and a low knife hand block to the front with the right arm whilst looking north.

18 *Han Son Joong Dan Mahk Kee*
Step forwards to the north with the right foot into front stance. Execute a right arm knife hand middle block whilst bringing the left fist to the left side.

19 *Joong Dan Kong Kyuk*
Step forwards to the north with the left foot into front stance and execute a left arm middle punch.

20 *Tro Joong Dan Kong Kyuk*
Still facing the north and in the same stance, execute a reverse middle punch with the right arm.

21 Preparation movement
Pull the left foot back so both feet are together with the knees straightened. Simultaneously bring both fists to the left side of the body (right palm facing down, left palm facing up) at the same level and hip twist whilst looking north.

22 *Bahk Ye Seo Ahn Euro Mahk Go Cha Kee*
From the previous position, execute a blocking outside to inside kick with the right foot.

23 *Sang Dan/Joong Dan Kong Kyuk*
Step forwards with the right leg into left leg back stance, simultaneously executing a high punch with the left arm and a middle punch with the right arm (both elbows slightly bent), whilst looking north.

㉔ Preparation movement
Pull the right foot back so both feet are together with the knees straightened. Simultaneously bring both fists to the right side of the body (left palm facing down, right palm facing up) at the same level and hip twist whilst looking north.

㉕ Bahk Ye Seo Ahn Euro Mahk Go Cha Kee
From the previous position, execute a blocking outside to inside kick with the left foot.

㉖ Sang Dan/Joong Dan Kong Kyuk
Step forwards with the left leg into right leg back stance. Simultaneously execute a high punch with the right arm and a middle punch with the left arm (both elbows slightly bent), whilst looking north.

㉗ Preparation movement
Pull the left foot back so both feet are together with the knees straightened. Simultaneously bring both fists to the left side of the body (right palm facing down, left palm facing up) at the same level and hip twist whilst looking north.

㉘ Bahk Ye Seo Ahn Euro Mahk Go Cha Kee
From the previous position, execute a blocking outside to inside kick with the right foot.

㉙ Sang Dan/Joong Dan Kong Kyuk
Step forwards with the right leg into left leg back stance. Simultaneously execute a high punch with the left arm and a middle punch with the right arm (both elbows slightly bent), whilst looking north.

30 *Tu Joo Mok/ Kong Kyuk*
Look to the left, pivot 180° to the left to face south and drop the right knee to the ground with the left foot flat. At the same time, execute a right arm uppercut and a left arm attack over the right shoulder.

31 *E Dan*
From the previous position, jump up with both feet in the air and twist the body 270° to the left, in preparation for a double knife hand middle block.

32 *Sang Soo Joong Dan Soo Do Mahk Kee*
Land with the right leg forwards in left leg back stance and execute a double knife hand middle block with the right arm.

33 *Sang Soo Ha Dan Soo Do Mahk Kee [Ki-ahp]*
Step backwards into right leg back stance, execute a double knife hand low block and **shout.**

Ba-ro Jase
Pull the left leg back and into ready stance.

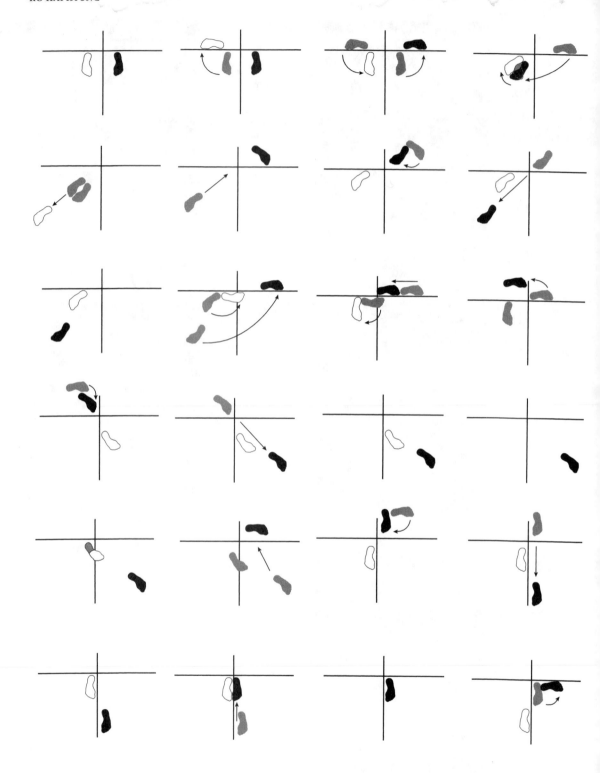

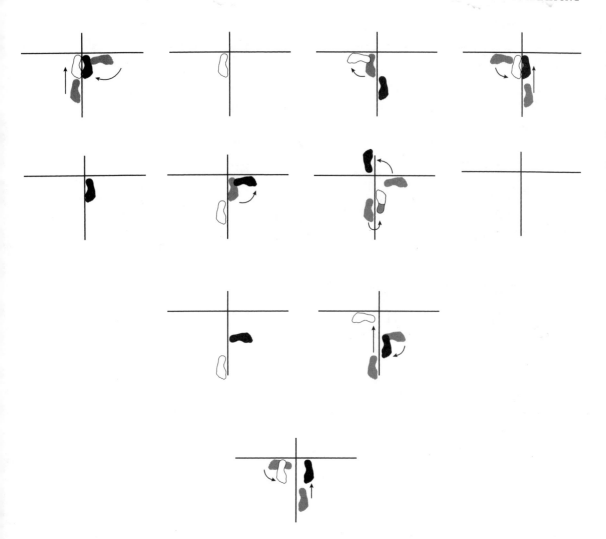

Sparring

Sparring has a strong code of conduct; practitioners must show discipline and control when practising attacking and defensive moves and must demonstrate their knowledge of the stances and basic movements.

Three-step sparring

Having just learned the basic steps and movements, the students put them into practice by executing in turn three forward attacks and three basic defence steps backwards.

One-step sparring

This is for advanced students who are skilled in three-step sparring; the students practise the correct attacking and defensive moves but take just one step forwards or backwards.

Il Soo Shik Dae Ryun – One-step sparring

Figure 1

Figure 2

Figure 3

Figure 1

Figure 2

Figure 3

Figure 1

Figure 2

Figure 3

Figure 1

Figure 2

Figure 3

Figure 4

Figure 1

Figure 2

Figure 3

Figure 4

Figure 1

Figure 2

Figure 3

Figure 4

Figure 5

Free sparring

Free sparring allows the students to move freely using combinations of attacking and defensive moves. Although the students may have achieved a high grade, the emphasis is still on practising basic movements and stances.

Hand and foot conditioning

Hard boards, pads and sandbags can be used to condition the hands and feet. It is essential to use the correct punching and kicking techniques as practised in forms and basic movements.

Figure 1

Figure 2

Figure 3

Figure 4

Figure 5

Figure 6

Figure 7

Sitting one-step sparring

From sitting position (**fig.1**) the attacker steps forwards into kneeling position and delivers a reverse punch; the defender immediately steps forwards with one leg and executes an inside to outside knife hand block and punches to the attacker's face (**fig.2**).

Figure 1

Figure 2

SITTING ONE-STEP SPARRING

From sitting position (fig.1) the
attacker steps forwards into kneeling position and delivers a punch;
the defender steps forwards and
executes an inside to outside kneeling position knife hand block
(fig.2). The defender grabs the wrist
of the offending hand, and twists it,
simultaneously striking and hyperextending the elbow (fig.3).

Figure 1

Figure 2

Figure 3

242

From sitting position (fig.1) the offender lunges forwards with a punch in a squatting position, and the defender quickly leans backwards, supporting the body with the elbow, and executes a side kick (fig.2).

Figure 1

Figure 2

Self-defence

The attacker grabs the hair of the defender from the front (fig.1). The defender grabs the attacking hand firmly with both hands (fig.2) and pulls backwards sharply into low front stance, hyperextending the attacker's wrist (fig.3).

Figure 1

Figure 2

Figure 3

The attacker grabs the collar of the defender (fig.1). The defender reaches over the top of the offending hand and places his thumb between the thumb and the forefinger of the attacker (fig.2), exerting pressure. The defender twists the offending hand, exerting pressure on the elbow (fig.3).

Figure 1

Figure 2

Figure 3

The attacker holds the defender in a bear hug from the back (fig.1). The defender stamps on the foot of the attacker and drops into horse stance, simultaneously raising the elbows upwards to break the grip (fig.2). The defender side steps, executes an elbow attack to the solar plexus, grabs the wrist of one of the attacker's hands with the free hand (fig.3) and executes a levering motion extending the attacker's elbow (fig.4).

Figure 1

Figure 2

Figure 3

Figure 4

The attacker grips the defender's wrists (fig.1). The defender steps forwards with one leg, simultaneously moving the hand to one side and allowing one of the hands to escape between the thumb and the forefinger (fig.2), and delivers a back fist/upper cut strike (fig.3).

Figure 1

Figure 2

Figure 3

The attacker grabs the defender's wrist (fig.1). The defender executes an inside to outside rotating movement, simultaneously grabbing the offending hand (fig.2). He then steps forwards, striking the elbow of the offending arm (fig.3).

Figure 1

Figure 2

Figure 3

The attacker grabs the defender's belt/waist (fig.1). The defender grabs the wrist of the offending hand tightly (fig.2), and with the free hand strikes the attacker's elbow, stepping forwards at the same time and locking/hyperextending the elbow (fig.3).

Figure 1

Figure 2

Figure 3

Group of participants and officials from Australia, Canada, Germany, Greece, Malaysia, United Kingdom and the United States at the 7th International Tang Soo Do Championships held in Malaysia (11 October 1997)

(Seated l-r): Masters J Michkofsky, E Vermes, B Y H Chew, S Carder, S Wallace, W P Tiong, N Zouraris, C N Lee, R Woodiwiss, J M H Tang, F Scott, S H Tay, P V M Chin, Grand Master Kang Uk Lee (President), T F K Ng, T Metaxas, I C H Tnay, P S Chong, E Titus, T T P Liew, J Y W Chin, Y K Chew, G Rickard, S Tilley, M C L Fong, T Wasylyk, G Petroski, W Ott

250

Glossary

English to Korean

Ancient name of the martial art in Korea
  Soo Bahk Do
Assistant Instructor Kyo Sa Nim
Attack Kong Kyuk
Attention Cha Ryut
Arm Pal

Back fist Kwon Do
Back kick Dwee Cha Kee
Back spinning chop kick Dwee Dull Ryo
  Chit-Go Cha Kee
Back stance Hu Gul Jase
Balance Jung Shim
Basic Kee Cho
Begin Shi-jak
Beginner Cho Bo Ja
Belt Dee
Between mouth & nose In Joong
Block Mahk Kee
Bow Kyung Yet
Breaking techniques Kyok Pa
By the count Ku Ryung Ae Mat Cho So

Circular inside to outside kick Ahn Ye Seo Bahk
  Euro Cha Kee
Circular outside to inside kick Bahk Ye Seo Ahn
  Euro Cha Kee
Circular outside to inside block kick Bahk Ye Seo
  Ahn Euro Mah-Go Cha Kee
Count Ku Ryung

Dan holder You Dan Ja
Degree/Holder of the midnight blue belt Dan
Diagonal inside to outside snap kick Peet Cha Kee
Duck foot stance Bal Bul Ri Go Mao Sogi Jase

Eight Yo-dol
Eighth Pal
Elbow Pal Koop
Elbow attack Pal Koop Kong Kyuk/Chi Kee
External power Weh Kung

Fifth Oh
First Il
Five Ta-sot
Focus of eyes Shi Sun

Foot techniques Jok Kee
Forefist Joong Kwon
Fore knuckle hand Ban Jul Kwan Soo
Form Hyung
Four Net
Fourth Sa
Free sparring Ja Yoo Dae Ryun
Front kick Ap Cha Kee
Front outer side of foot Bal Ahp Buri Yup
Front pushing kick Ap Mee Ro Cha Kee
Front snap kick Ap Podo Cha Kee
Front stance Chon Gool Jase

Grade (colour belt) Gup
Grand Master/Chief Instructor Kwan Jang Nim
Gup holder You Gup Ja

Hammer fist Kap Kwon
Hand techniques Soo Kee
Heel Bal Dwee Koom Chi
High block Sang Dan Mahk Kee
High punch Sang Dan Kong Kyuk
High section Sang Dan
High section knife hand block Soo Do Sang Dan
  Mahk Kee
Horse stance Kee Mahk Jase

Inside to outside block Ahn Ye Seo Bahk Euro
  Mahk Kee
Instep Bal Deung
Internal power Neh Kung

Jumping (all jumping kicks start with this term)
  E Dan
Junior member Hu Beh

Kick Cha Kee
Knee Moo Roop
Knee attack Moo Roop Cha Kee
Knee turning round house kick Moo Roop Dull
  Ryo Cha Kee
Knife hand Soo Do

Left Wen Jok
Leg Ta Ri
Low back stance Chwe Ha Dan Jase

Low block   Ha Dan Mahk Kee
Low section   Ha Dan
Low section knife hand block   Soo Do Ha Dan
   Mahk Kee

Meditation   Muk Nyum
Middle punch front stance   Joong Dan Kong
   Kyuk
Middle section   Joong Dan
Middle section knife hand block   Soo Do Joong
   Dan Mahk Kee

Name of the art we study   Tang Soo Do
Name of the style/organisation   Moo Duk Kwan
National flag   Kuk Gi
Nine   A-hop
Ninth   Ku

One   Ha-na
One finger fist   Il Ji Kwon
One finger spear hand   Il Ji Kwon Soo
One-step sparring   Il Soo Shik Dae Ryun
Organisation flag   Kwan Gi
Outside to inside block   Bahk Ye Seo Ahn Euro
   Mahk Kee

Palm foot   Bal Ba Dak Mit
Palm heel   Son Ba Dak Mit (Jang Kwon)
Plier hand   Jip Kye Shon
Prefect   Ban Jang

Qualified Instructor from 4th Dan upwards
   Sa Bom Nim

Ready   Joon Bee
Ready for kick   Bal Cha Kee Joon Bee
Ready stance   Joon Bee Jase
Relax   Shio
Return   Ba-ro
Reverse punch, back stance   Yuk Jin Kong Kyuk
Reverse inside to outside block   Tro Ahn Ye Seo
   Bahk Euro Mahk Kee
Reverse outside to inside block   Tro Bahk Ye Seo
   Ahn Euro Mahk Kee
Ridge hand/Reverse knife hand   Yuk Soo Do
Right   O Rin Jok
Round-house kick   Dull Ryo Cha Kee

Second   Ee
Self-defence   Ho Sin Sul/Bo Shin Bop
Senior Dan holder   Ko Dan Ja
Senior member   Sun Beh
Seven   Il-gop
Seventh   Chil
Shout   Ki-hap
Side heel   Bal Yup Koom Chi

Side hook kick   Yup Hu Ri Kee
Side kick   Yup Cha Kee
Side of heel under the foot   Bal Dwee Koom
   Chi Yup Ba Dak
Side punch (side) horse stance   Hoeng Jin Kong
   Kyuk
Side snap kick   Yup Podo Cha Kee
Side stamping kick   Bahl Yup Chit Pal Kee
Side stance   Sa Goh Rip Jase
Sit   Chak Sut
Six   Yo-sot
Sixth   Yuk
Soft fist   Yoo Kwon
Sparring   Dae Ryun
Spear hand   Kwan Soo
Spear hand attack   Kwan Soo Kong Kyuk
Spinning back kick   Dwee Dull Ryo Cha Kee
Spiritual power   Kung
Stamping kick   Chit Bal Kee
Sitting sparring   Chwa Dae Ryun
Student member   Kwan Won

Ten   Yol
Tenth   Ship
Three   Set
Three-step sparring   Sam Soo Shik Dae Ryun
Third   Sam
Training hall   Do Jang
Training uniform   Do Balk
Turn   Tora
Turn to rear   Dwee Ro Tora
Two   Tul
Two finger spear hand   Ee Ji Kwan Soo
Two fist (X) high block   Sang Soo Sang Dan
   Mahk Kee
Two fist (X) low block   Sang Soo Ha Dan
   Mahk Kee
Two fist middle block   Sang Soo Joong Dan
   Mahk Kee

Upper wrist technique   Son Mok Deung

Without the count   Ku Ryung Op Shi
Wrist   Pal Mok

Korean to English

A-hop   Nine
Ahn Ye Seo Bahk Euro Cha Kee   Circular inside to outside kick
Ahn Ye Seo Bahk Euro Mahk Kee   Inside to outside block
Ap Cha Kee   Front kick
Ap Mee Ro Cha Kee   Front pushing kick
Ap Podo Cha Kee   Front snap kick

Ba-ro   Return
Bahk Ye Seo Ahn Euro Cha Kee   Circular outside to inside kick
Bahk Ye Seo Ahn Euro Mah-Go Cha Kee   Circular outside to inside block kick
Bahk Ye Seo Ahn Euro Mahk Kee   Outside to inside block
Bahl Yup Chit Pal Kee   Side stamping kick
Bal Ahp Buri Yup   Front outer side of foot
Bal Ba Dak Mit   Palm foot
Bal Bul Ri Go Mao Sogi Jase   Duck foot stance
Bal Cha Kee Joon Bee   Ready for kick
Bal Deung   Instep
Bal Dwee Koom Chi   Heel
Bal Dwee Koom Chi Yup Ba Dak   Side of heel under the foot
Bal Yup Koom Chi   Side heel
Ban Jang   Prefect
Ban Jul Kwan Soo   Fore knuckle hand

Cha Kee   Kick
Cha Ryut   Attention
Chak Sut   Sit
Chil   Seventh
Chit Bal Kee   Stamping kick
Cho Bo Ja   Beginner
Chon Gool Jase   Front stance
Chwa Dae Ryun   Sitting sparring
Chwe Ha Dan Jase   Low back stance

Dan   Degree/Holder of the midnight blue belt
Dae Ryun   Sparring
Dee   Belt
Do Balk   Training uniform
Do Jang   Training hall
Dull Ryo Cha Kee   Round house kick
Dwee Cha Kee   Back kick
Dwee Dull Ryo Cha Kee   Spinning back kick
Dwee Dull Ryo Chit-Go Cha Kee   Back spinning chop kick
Dwee Ro Tora   Turn to rear

E Dan   Jumping (all jumping kicks start with this term)
Ee   Second

Ee Ji Kwan Soo   Two finger spear hand

Gup   Grade (colour belt)

Ha-na   One
Ha Dan   Low section
Ha Dan Mahk Kee   Low block
Ho Sin Sul   Self-defence
Hoeng Jin Kong Kyuk   Side punch (side) horse stance
Hu Beh   Junior member
Hu Gul Jase   Back stance
Hyung   Form

Il   First
Il-gop   Seven
Il Ji Kwon   One finger fist
Il Ji Kwon Soo   One finger spear hand
Il Soo Shik Dae Ryun   One-step sparring
In Joong   Between mouth & nose

Ja Yoo Dae Ryun   Free sparring
Jip Kye Shon   Plier hand
Jok Kee   Foot techniques
Joon Bee   Ready
Joon Bee Jase   Ready stance
Joong Dan   Middle section
Joong Dan Kong Kyuk   Middle punch front stance
Joong Kwon   Forefist
Jung Shim   Balance

Kap Kwon   Backfist
Kee Cho   Basic
Kee Mahk Jase   Horse stance
Ki-hap   Shout
Ko Dan Ja   Senior Dan holder
Kong Kyuk   Attack
Ku   Ninth
Ku Ryung   Count
Ku Ryung Ae Mat Cho So   By the count
Ku Ryung Op Shi   Without the count
Kuk Gi   Korean National flag
Kung   Spiritual power
Kwan Gi   Organisational flag
Kwan Jang Nim   Grand Master/Chief Instructor
Kwan Soo   Spear hand
Kwan Soo Kong Kyuk   Spear hand attack
Kwan Won   Student member
Kwon Do   Hammer fist
Kyo Sa Nim   Assistant instructor
Kyok Pa   Breaking techniques
Kyung Yet   Bow

Mahk Kee   Block
Moo Duk Kwan   Name of the style/organisation
Moo Roop   Knee
Moo Roop Cha Kee   Knee attack
Moo Roop Dull Ryo Cha Kee   Knee turning
   round house kick
Muk Nyum   Meditation

Neh Kung   Internal power
Net   Four

O Rin Jok   Right
Oh   Fifth

Pal   Arm
Pal Mok   Wrist
Pahl   Eighth
Pal Koop   Elbow
Pal Koop Kong Kyuk   Elbow attack
Peet Cha Kee   Diagonal inside to outside snap kick

Sa Bom Nim   Qualified instructor from 4th Dan
   upwards
Sa Goh Rip Jase   Side stance
Sa   Fourth
Sam   Third
Sam Soo Shik Dae Ryun   Three-step sparring
Sang Dan   High section
Sang Dan Mahk Kee   High block
Sang Dan Kong Kyuk   High punch
Sang Soo Ha Dan Mahk Kee   Two fist (X) low
   block
Sang Soo Joong Dan Mahk Kee   Two fist middle
   block
Sang Soo Sang Dan Mahk Kee   Two fist (X)
   high block
Set   Three
Shi-Jak   Begin
Shi Sun   Focus of eyes
Ship   Tenth
Shio   Relax
Soo Bahk Do   Ancient name of the martial art
   in Korea
Soo Do   Knife hand
Soo Do Ha Dan Mahk Kee   Low section knife
   hand block
Soo Do Joong Dan Mahk Kee   Middle section
   knife hand block
Soo Do Sang Dan Mahk Kee   High section
   knife hand block
Soo Kee   Hand techniques
Son Ba Dak Mit (Jang Kwon)   Palm heel
Son Mok Deung   Upper wrist technique
Sun Beh   Senior member

Ta Ri   Leg
Ta-sot   Five
Tang Soo Do   Name of the art we study
Tora   Turn
Tro Ahn Ye Seo Bahk Euro Mahk Kee   Reverse
   inside to outside block
Tro Bahk Ye Seo Ahn Euro Mahk Kee   Reverse
   outside to inside block
Tul   Two

Weh Kung   External power
Wen Jok   Left

Yo-dol   Eight
Yo-sot   Six
Yol   Ten
Yoo Kwon   Soft fist
You Dan Ja   Dan holder
You Gup Ja   Gup holder
Yuk   Sixth
Yuk Jin Kong Kyuk   Reverse punch, back stance
Yuk Soo Do   Ridge/Reverse knife hand
Yup Cha Kee   Side kick
Yup Hu Ri Kee   Side hook kick
Yup Podo Cha Kee   Side snap kick

Bibliography

		Extract
Cho Sun Il Bo Newspaper **(Tang Soo) Do**	*Ah! Koguryo* Culture 2 Section 1994	Soo Bahk Dae Ryun Jase
Dr Chun Ho Tae	*A Mural Painting of Koguryo Ancient Tomb* K.B.S. Korea Communication Broadcast 1994	Deer Hunting
Dr Hwang Su Young	*Suk Gul Am* Youl Hwa Dang Publisher 1989	Kum Kang Yuk Sa
Dr Kang Woo Bang	*Korean Sculpture of Buddhism* Dea Won Sa Ltd 1995	Inside Suk Gul Am Kum Kang Yuk Sa
Dr Tae Hung Sup	*Korean Sculpture of Stone Carving* Mun Yea Publisher 1995	Bul Kuk Sa Chung Un Kyo

Group of Instructors with Grand Master Kang Uk Lee (President)

Front row (l-r): Masters E McGonigle, F F K Chin, S Tilley, C Bogeart, F Daniels, E Titus, I Busby, T Metaxas (Greece), P V M Chin (Secretary General), Grand Master K U Lee (President), S H Tay (Germany), J M H Tang (Treasurer), R Woodiwiss, D Griffiths, A Sukhnandan, J Meakins, S Carder, A S P Chin, D Allerton.

United Kingdom Tang Soo (Soo Bahk) Do Federation
Moo Duk Kwan
P. O. Box 184
Watford
Herts WD1 3LS